GOLDEN

ENLIGHTENMENT II

50+ Answers for Seekers of
Spiritual Knowledge, Truth and Wisdom

by

James

McQuitty

(Revised & Extended from Golden Enlightenment 1994)

DEDICATION

==

The publication of this book would not have been possible without the overwhelming support and kindness of a very rare lady, and for this, I give my special thanks, and dedicate this book to Mary Stuart-Thomas. God bless you.

ISBN 0 9534532 0 0

Published by James McQuitty
36 Alfred Street
Ryde
Isle of Wight
PO33 2TS

Printed in Great Britain

ACKNOWLEDGEMENTS

Two people in particular helped to inspire this edition with their encouragement, and by asking valuable questions, I thank most sincerely Verena Cayley and Dave Blight for their love and friendship. While I also acknowledge the help and inspiration I feel privileged to receive from spirit world guides and friends. Also deserving of the thanks I offer are many teachers, far too many to name, from the physical pathway. Additionally, for their support, I thank the Spiritualists of Lewisham and Worthing, Ann Dutt and David G. Wright.

CONTENTS

===

CHAPTER THREE: SUFFERING

CHAPTER FOUR: RELIGIOUS

CHAPTER FIVE: SPIRITUAL

CHAPTER SIX: ODDS & CURIOS

CHAPTER SEVEN: OPENING THE MIND

ABOUT THE AUTHOR

==

My name is James John McQuitty, I was born on 2 December 1950, in Putney, London. Currently I am a writer and a practicing channel for Spiritual healing. I am also a seeker of truth, although I freely admit that I still have much to learn, for as one aspect of truth unfolds another which needs explanation is glimpsed, and in this way we are all guided forward.

I do not remember a great many incidents of a psychic or spiritual nature occurring during my formative years, but a couple are worthy of recount. The first of which occurred when I was around eleven years of age; during an accidental collision with a motorcycle I was propelled upward from my bicycle, and while in mid-air it seemed as though time stood-still, for I was halfway through a somersault when everything appeared to freeze; and it was as though I heard a voice say something like: "stay calm and complete this somersault like a school gymnastic exercise, and you will be all right". I managed to do as instructed and landed upon my feet without injury, and for years after thought little more about the incident; in much the same way as many other children who, having experienced phenomena, just accept it as natural.

Another incident, or series of incidences, occurred when I was around the age of fourteen or fifteen years. Like most teenagers I loved the modern music of the time, such as the marvellous melodies produced by the Beatles; and I often stayed in my bedroom, even in the cold of winter, with no such luxuries as central heating, while I listened to records. I used to think how easy it would be to write the words for songs, and would often mentally construct my own songs with words and tunes echoing within my mind. To my amazement, I then began to hear the very songs which I considered I had mentally constructed, being broadcast upon the radio. I was always reasonably rational in my thinking, so wondered whether I had heard the songs before, and having forgotten, only copied them. But this became an impossibility, when once again a song I had 'imagined' only a night or two earlier, was played one morning on the radio, after which the disc-jockey announced "for the very first-time on radio" and further said "a new release". For a time I thought someone was 'tuning-in' to my mind and stealing my ideas; but the phenomena soon faded, and has never since repeated. What I now understand to have happened, is that *I* was the one 'tuning-in' to some frequency of the ether, or the 'unofficial' air waves of thought which surround this planet, and hearing songs which were being prepared for release.

At sixteen years of age, out of curiosity and a desire to know whether there truly was life after 'death', which no adult I had ever met at that stage in my life seemed to dare question or consider, I made my first visit to witness a medium demonstrate, to prove life after 'death'. In her messages she gave such clear evidential proof of survival, to so many of those in attendance, and all given freely with love and without monetary gain, that I was totally convinced of the genuine nature of what had been presented.

An occasional spiritual link was around me during the 1970's, such as a friendly push on my shoulder as I crossed Peckham Rye, in London, which I somehow knew was from my Grandfather; and the sudden feeling of what I can only describe as euphoria, total elation and well-being, overwhelming me, when I knew *All* (of the unseen reality and all which really matters) is at peace, in harmony, and of beauty.

However, it was 1980 before my real spiritual awakening began, for while employed in Saudi Arabia I truly discovered the power of prayer. It was after witnessing an Egyptian work colleague enjoying the use of his prayer mat, that I was inspired to try prayer for myself. For I was feeling in need of some upliftment, when, with the memory of the Egyptian still in my mind, I came across an old unused prayer mat, and decided to give prayer a try. The spiritual upliftment I received was immediate, so from that time forward, I began to make use of prayer whenever I felt the need.

Upon my return to England, early in 1981, I began to seriously renew my quest for spiritual knowledge; when by coincidence, or guidance, I found that each week mediumship was being demonstrated not too far from where I lived. Amazingly, it transpired to be the same medium whom I had seen when sixteen years of age, who was the demonstrator. Her name was Jessie Nason, and she was a master of her craft, and even though she was happy and willing to demonstrate to the smallest group in any size room or hall, she was so renowned for her ability that she had, upon invitation, successfully demonstrated in the Royal Albert Hall in London. Such was her fame, capability, standing and status in the field of mediumship, she became the first medium in history to demonstrate clairvoyance on British television, when she appeared on the David Frost Show; then went on to appear in Ireland, on the Gay Byrne, Late Late Show, with great success on both occasions.[1] Although when I began to attend Jessie's weekly demonstrations, I knew none of this, and it was years later before I realised I had started my investigations by observing one of the finest mediums in the country.

Jessie was the first medium to supply me with personal and conclusive proof of survival, when she 'reunited' me with a departed Grandfather, she also correctly foretold who my next employers were to be, and she was also the first to suggest that I too could develop spiritual gifts.

Over the years which have followed I have attended hundreds of demonstrations, given by almost as many different mediums, in various parts of the country, and only on very rare occasions could I dismiss the information passed as totally inconclusive. I have received hundreds of personal messages at public demonstrations, and many more during private sittings, some with mediums of fame and high repute within the Spiritualist movement. As far back as 1982 I was even given messages that I should be writing, and was told I would receive inspirational help, and I tested this one night before sleep by asking for proof, and just as I was about to fall asleep I received an entire script suitable for television in one amazing inspirational flash, I wrote down as much as I could remember, but have never drafted it properly.

Again, this time in 1991, during a sitting with an entranced friend, when I asked what I should be doing, her guide told me I should be writing, and she, the entranced friend, knew nothing of my much earlier message. This time I decided to take heed of the advice, and upon moving to Ryde in 1992 to find peace away from the big city rat-race, I began to put my first tentative thoughts and ideas on paper, and this led to the first version of *Golden Enlightenment*.

At the time of writing this, consciously, I experience only fleeting communication, and am predominantly used as a healing channel; although I'm told that ideas and thoughts to help with my writing are passed to me in the form of 'mind-waves'.

12

I have since 1986 seen spirit world visitors on many occasions, the first such appearance having taken place in the Forest Hill area of London where, at that time, I was living. It was during the early hours one morning when a noise woke me, and I saw a spirit lady walk clean through my closed bedroom door, she proceeded to look around, before vanishing from my limited psychic vision. This was repeated the very next night, but on this occasion it was a younger spirit lady. Some of my friends, who are also practicing mediums for communication, told me there were spirits who visited that particular house, but the spirit visitors never bothered me, and in a way their presence was reassuring, for I consider it to have been my privilege to have seen first those two ladies, and over the years since, many more spirit visitors, guides and helpers, as well as several spirit animals. On occasions, during the middle of the night, I also hear spirit bells, and this phenomena was predicted by a medium several weeks before it began.

As I have said, I appreciated the spirits who visited the house in Forest Hill, and I suppose I must have met with their approval, which is more than can be said for a friend of mine, as the following account details. In the house just mentioned, I had a party which ran into the early hours of the next morning, and a male friend made use of a spare bedroom for the night; but unfortunately his presence did not meet with the approval of my spirit visitors. For in the dark early hours I woke to hear a noise downstairs, and upon investigation found my guest trapped between the locked porch and front doors. He said he had got up to visit the lavatory, which was next to his bedroom, when a spirit gentleman grabbed him by the neck and marched him downstairs, opened the door, and pushed him outside, while saying *they* didn't want him in the house. He never stayed again!

A series of messages which I received from several different mediums, over the course of two or three years, did cause me some confusion; for I was told of a twin Brother in the spirit world, who would one day give his name, and my Mother knew nothing about him. Some time later I cleared up the mystery when I received confirmation through an entranced medium that my Brother is called *White Cloud*, and that plans for his intended birth as my twin, which we had been on a number of previous occasions during past incarnations, had this time been changed; with him on this occasion choosing to stay in the spirit world to act as my guide. I have been told about some of the past lives we have shared, including one as girls, thousands of years ago, when we were training in a special temple where we were learning about sound vibrations, but passed during an earthquake.

The name *White Cloud* has since been confirmed to me on many occasions, and I have even heard him personally talk, through another entranced medium. My partner has also channelled information concerning him, and both of our lives together as members of the Apache tribe. When I was known as *Silver Birch*, and my partner as *Little White Bear*, whose Sister, who has also communicated, was known as *Little White Cloud*.

Some of what I have said may not be satisfactory evidence to convince those who do not wish to believe, or even those who would like conclusive proof of eternal life; as the written word can never fully achieve this. But suffice it to say, if any reader should earnestly and truthfully seek, they will find communication is not only possible, but is occurring every single day, all over the world. One only has to allow those in the spirit world the opportunity, and right conditions to communicate, for them to do so.

Over the years I have also studied written spiritual teachings, including those of many past and present mediums, along with the highly informative teachings of wisdom received from those who are living within the spiritual realms. When such information is combined with personal evidence and experiences, producing a corroborated understanding, I believe the final conclusions make a good basis for presenting the contents of this book as *spiritual knowledge, truth and wisdom.*

FOREWORD

===

The intention behind the construction of the original *Golden Enlightenment* was to provide readers with simple, easy to understand answers, to the questions asked by most people when they first embark upon their quest for spiritual knowledge, truth and wisdom. It was intended as a beginners handbook. While this revised and extended version, which encapsulates the earlier version along with a good number more questions will, I trust, prove of value to not only 'beginners', to whom I believe it will still prove of value, but also to those who might regard themselves a little further along the spiritual pathway, while throughout I have endeavoured to ensure that it retains its easy to understand explanation.

The answers I have given express the truth as I presently perceive it to be; this does not mean my understanding is complete, for our concept of truth is always developing and seeking new ways to find expression. Since 1981, when I first began to seriously study and investigate spiritual truths, I have found many answers, expressed in a variety of ways; some have seemed simple, some very complicated, but all leading to the same underlying truth, that all people come from the same divine source, and are eternally linked, as individualised aspects of God. With the passing we call death being merely a step forward, onto another plane or level of existence, where in reality death does not exist.

Once read, I hope this book will provide a foundation which will help each reader to move forward with greater confidence, understanding more of their own spiritual nature, and thus helping their eternal growth toward enlightenment. As the contents pages show, the format of this book is in question and answer style, making it easy to find and read again any question of particular concern or interest; the first chapter details the facts and circumstances surrounding survival, which is guaranteed and automatic for all people. Here readers will learn what to expect upon their own eventual passing, detailing how they will be met and helped, very often by loved ones who have gone ahead, or otherwise by friends or guides, who will take them forward to their new home.

The survival chapter also deals with the question of children who pass, and the fact their progress is assured, with their age, or stage of development at passing, not affecting or hindering their spiritual growth and progression. With survival, or as it should really be considered: continuance of life, being assured for all, the question of what happens to those who pass by their own actions, by suicide, is also answered. With reassurance for all who have lost someone in this manner, that there is no punishment or damnation awaiting anyone passing in this way, rather they are treated with sympathy, compassion and love. The animal kingdom is not excluded, and I detail how pets too enjoy their new life, in the eternal realms of the spirit world. Where they are cared for, and are eventually reunited with those who have love for them.

In chapter two readers will find answers of a more personal and philosophical nature; detailing such as the greater freedom of choice they will enjoy upon their eventual passing to the spirit world, and the reason why they were born in the first place. Also included in this chapter is the truth surrounding the so-called day of Judgment, which is needlessly feared by so many, who have been wrongly taught to live in fear of such a day. In this same chapter I also answer a question to put many minds at ease, concerning those who have married twice, or taken another partner, after losing the previous love of their life. For those who are apprehensive about how their life will proceed in the spirit world, having had more than one partner, and love, my answer will I'm sure bring release from worry.

Chapter three deals with suffering, including the reasons why some people might actually volunteer to be born to a life which will involve their suffering, and how this is sometimes undertaken to teach aspects of suffering or compassion to others. I also offer hope, with words to bring comfort to those recently bereaved; and discuss the controversial subject of euthanasia.

Religious considerations are aired in chapter four, including why so much spiritual knowledge is suppressed by so many of the orthodox world religions, along with an explanation of why the image of God is believed to be reflected through mankind. Also in this chapter are further details concerning the factual existence of heaven, the spirit world, and the answer to whether a domain called hell actually exists; and, I also give what I believe to be a truer understanding of the meaning of sin. To conclude this chapter: I give my opinion on the true status, worth and purpose, during his life on earth, of the man known as Jesus; along with the understanding of a highly evolved guide, who communicated from the spirit world.

In the fifth, and spiritual chapter, I endeavour to explain why some people: such as the majority of those who teach orthodox religious beliefs, fear spiritual communication and knowledge. Amongst the many questions covered in this chapter, is the explanation of how mediums are able to communicate, and how some of them can be channels for amazing phenomena, such as the materialisation of objects, or spirit world people, while others can draw portraits of visiting relatives, or guides, whose

18

lives upon earth may have been lived many thousands of years ago. The consequences and fact of reincarnation is also considered, as well as the question of whether some upon this planet might actually be new-born souls, living their very first life in human form. I also explain what the word karma means, and how its effects can have far reaching consequences, which can even have repercussions which extend to future incarnations. Spirit world guides and guardian angels are also differentiated between, with their different roles identified; while the description of eternal life in the numerous levels of the spirit world might inspire and catch the imagination of many readers. Consideration is also given in this chapter to the development of personal gifts, the power of prayer, and the benefits which are possible through the application of Spiritual healing.

Chapter six covers a range of interesting questions, one of which concerns the merits of meditation, while another considers the possible advantages of positive thinking. Additionally, in this chapter readers will find information and advice which could prove invaluable and possibly beneficial to their health, while also improving their quality of life.

The final chapter encourages readers to open their minds still further, to vastly greater possibilities than they might have previously dared to dream. For amongst other answers I include here my opinion as to whether there actually is life upon other planets, and what the arrival of other planetary beings might mean to us all; while the very purpose to creation is contemplated.

I close with a brief summary, together with my final thoughts, which I believe will leave readers feeling encouraged and excited. To help readers who are new to this subject, I have additionally produced what I believe will prove a useful glossary, and a list of suggested reading. Finally, to every reader, may I wish happiness and joy, and may the love of God shine in your hearts, and eternally in every thought, word and deed of your never-ending lives.

Chapter One

SURVIVAL

Questions 1-6

==

1. DO WE ALL SURVIVE 'DEATH'?

We can do no other than survive 'death'---because in reality 'death' does not exist---it is simply the shedding of our physical form; we are not simply physical beings, we are first and foremost spiritual beings, who are eternal and indestructible aspects of God. Our physical form is only the temporary housing for our spirit, while we live our current incarnation upon earth. Our physical body fulfils a purpose: it allows our spirit within to undertake a series of lessons which are contained within experiences, lessons which can only be learned while we are in a physical body. But it is only designed for a limited time span, a length of time suitable for us to experience whichever lessons we came to learn, then to be left behind.

At the same time as we live and experience through our physical body and its senses: we are spiritual beings, we do not suddenly acquire a spiritual body upon 'death', we have one all the time. Our spiritual body is linked to our physical body, and it is this spiritual aspect of our being which motivates our physical body to live. In fact, we can only exist upon the earth, in a physical form, because of the motivating power of our spirit within. When our spirit decides it has experienced and learned all it came for, it begins to withdraw, and the connection it has with our physical body gradually weakens, until it is finally broken, causing the death of our physical form.

Our spirit, or spiritual body, cannot be seen with normal physical eyes because it vibrates at a frequency which is much faster than that of the physical plane of existence. In fact we each have several finer energy bodies which connect to our physical body, with each operating on a slightly different frequency to the other, forming a link between our physical and our higher spiritual body. They create a vibrational bridge, from our spirit, down through our higher-self (or higher-mind), mental, emotional (astral or elemental), and etheric (or vital), to our physical body. Some or all of these finer energy bodies can sometimes be seen by clairvoyants: in the form of an aura around our physical body; with the amount which can be seen, and perhaps understood, dependent upon the development and personal knowledge of the clairvoyant.

During physical life these finer energy bodies register every thought, word and deed, and store and relay the information to our higher self (or higher mind); and upon 'death' no scrap of information, no thought, no experience, is lost. Our mind: which is the consciousness of our spirit, and infinitely superior to our brain, continues to function, and is capable of remembering everything of importance or value which occurred during incarnation. This allows each of us to be our own judge, when we come to review our physical life; for what is often called judgment day is really self-judgment, a time of review, with memories and experiences looked at from a spiritual perspective. In this way, each of us is able to see exactly what we have, or have not, gained from our lifetime.

Having found that our life has continued after 'death', and perhaps, but not necessarily having reviewed our incarnation,

22

we will be guided to the level, realm or sphere (these three terms are more or less interchangeable) of existence to match our attainment. This level will reflect our own level of consciousness, which in turn reflects our level of progression through our recently concluded incarnation, which is automatically added to the level we attained through previous incarnations, in other words our sum total of attainment. Through many incarnations we try to learn and progress a little further each time, and slowly reach higher and finer levels; the system of where we have earned the right to be is infallible, as our very being, our spirit, will vibrate at the level of consciousness or attainment we have reached.

In this way each of us will be drawn to the level which is right for us, and no higher or lower; this is a natural law of God which cannot be cheated or fooled; money or status upon earth having no bearing upon this, we can only receive or attain as we have earned. If we are kind, considerate, compassionate, honest to ourselves and to others, and try to express love in all of our dealings with others, we will be on the right path to attain to a higher level of the spirit world; while if we are greedy, selfish, rude and uncaring, expressing no compassion, friendship or love, we will find ourselves on a much lower level, when we eventually return to the spirit world.

2. WHEN WE PASS TO THE SPIRIT WORLD, WILL WE BE REUNITED WITH OUR LOVED ONES?

When we pass we will not only be reunited with our loved ones, it is likely they will come to meet us; for such a forthcoming event is usually known well in advance by those progressed in the spirit world, and they will pass the news of our intended passing to those of our loved ones who are already there. For even though there are many levels in the spirit world, a bond of love will always be encouraged and find expression; as love is one of the primary motivating forces of the spirit world and of all creation.

So even if our loved ones have progressed to higher levels than ourselves, if they desire to visit or stay with us they will be perfectly free and able to do so; and if the level attained by ourselves is higher, then we will be free to stay with our loved ones, if we so choose.

But of course if neither party wish to continue the relationship, each of us would be freely entitled to go our own way; for love unites if reciprocated, but if it is only one-sided, and the other party wished to be separate, then no force could compel co-operation.

We are of course all infinite spirit beings here and now, only currently functioning through our physical body, and since we are spirit we cannot be truly separated from loved ones; and we probably meet them on many occasions during sleep state, when our spirit is able to leave our physical body. This is basically the same process as 'death', except that during out-of-body sleep experiences a link is maintained with our physical body, keeping it alive, and allowing our spirit to return. If we re-enter our physical body too speedily, perhaps, for instance, because we are disturbed by noise, this can cause us to convulse (to jerk) as we wake, and is something most of us have experienced at some time.

Our brain, being a physical organ, is unfortunately unable to remember much, if any, of our sleep state meetings; sometimes a small fleeting recollection may register, and we often think of this as just a dream; but it is much more, and I can tell of meetings I have personally experienced with two relatives. The first was as long ago as 1984, and involved my uncle Alfred who, at that time, had recently passed; I have a clear memory of meeting him and of him telling me that his experience of passing, and still finding himself alive "was a bit of a shock at first", and he added "but I'm getting used to it now". I do not believe that before his passing he had any expectations of survival, and when he said it was a bit of a shock, I presume he meant a pleasant one. On a more recent occasion, during 1993, I again visited this same uncle, when he showed me a scroll concerning the history of his wife (who was an orphan of unknown parents), who by that time had also passed, and this fact suddenly came out in our conversation; then I remembered that my uncle had passed first, and this sort of realisation usually ends such an experience very quickly, bringing one back to their physical body and awakening. On this occasion it was almost the same, but before it ended my uncle gave me a very roguish and knowing smile, expressing pleasure at my realisation, and at having played a further part in my life.

Another such experience of a spirit world meeting, and even more recently, was with my Father, Stanley, two months after his passing in 1994; I was sitting talking to him and although I do not recall the earlier conversation it seemed we had been together for some time; then the realisation once more came to me that he had passed, and I was therefore 'out of body', and when I mentioned this to my Father his reaction was to smile and confirm the fact. But before being drawn back to my physical body, he managed to tell me how he had been watching my Mother, Elizabeth, just after his passing, and seen her tears, and he was chuckling, and saying how daft it was, inferring that since he was perfectly well and happy, tears where not necessary, and that ended the experience. So when we awake with such a memory we should rejoice, for even though the remembrance may be blurred and confused it is almost certain we were together, in the spirit world, with our loved ones.

3. DO CHILDREN GROW-UP IN THE SPIRIT WORLD?

All life continues after 'death', regardless of the age at the time of passing. So when a child or a baby of any age, even a miscarried or aborted child passes from the physical, spiritual growth continues. In the spirit world there are places of rest, and of learning, along with all the care and attention that could possibly be required by any individual; so the development, growth and happiness of any child is assured.

Development can be speedier than physical growth, depending upon the needs and the capacity of the spirit; and it is often said of a child who lived a short incarnation that "the child was an old soul" and this can be very true. For even the shortest life upon earth can be enough to teach the old soul the lesson or experience they came to undertake; and it is also possible the old soul did not return to learn for him or herself, they may simply have been helping a parent to undergo an experience the parent wished, on a higher level of consciousness, to learn from.

26

It is also true that an old soul may not need to grow-up, so to speak, as they are already a mature spirit; and they can if they so wish use the form of the body which was theirs during their short stay upon earth, and they may very well do so if they are in communication with parents and loved ones upon the earth; but if communication is not sought or necessary, the old soul may well revert to using an appearance from an earlier incarnation.

The term 'growth' can be very misleading, growth in a spiritual sense is experience, knowledge, understanding, progression, wisdom and much more. It is not the same as in the physical sense of growing-up or older, for spirit is eternal and therefore ageless; and in strict terms one cannot be an 'old soul' only a highly progressed or wise soul.

On occasions children, or those manifesting as children from the spirit world (and some spirits do choose to retain the appearance of a child) return to the earth plane of existence to make contact with children upon earth; they return as playmates and friends, and can often be fully seen and heard by earth children, for during the first seven years of life upon earth a much stronger link is maintained with the spirit world. When parents discourage their young children from acknowledging what they mistakenly believe to be imaginary playmates, they often cause a shutdown of their child's psychic or spiritual faculties, and thus severe their communication. If only all parents could understand the reality of the spirit world and the love with which the spirit children come, they would then feel privileged and delighted for their children; such parents also have a great opportunity, for their child is in fact acting as a natural medium, and if they took the opportunity to gently and sensibly ask questions, without becoming over-demanding upon such a link: which is primarily for the benefit of the child, they might gain interesting and perhaps useful information from their child's playmate.

4. WHAT HAPPENS TO THOSE WHO COMMIT SUICIDE?

Those who commit suicide will, whenever possible, be met and cared for in the same way in which all are cared for; there is no damnation or eternal punishment awaiting them. Usually those meeting them will be relatives or friends who love and care for them, otherwise it will be a guide or guides who also have love for them; and either way they will be comforted and treated with sympathy, compassion and encouragement. Often those who pass in this way have been crying out for help, but received none that was adequate for their needs while upon earth, heaven would hardly be heaven if those there also rejected them in any way. If any reader knows of someone who has passed in this way, send them love, through prayer, as this will help them to come to terms with their experience and recover from the anguish of it.

Those who commit suicide do not have to return to experience duplicate life circumstances which led to their passing; although, in time, they may wish to return and continue to experience and learn; for even in suicide, and the experiences which led to it, lessons are learned, perhaps not to the full capacity available, but none the less some aspects would have been learned.

The victim may of course suffer great remorse over their actions, and this will partially be a reflection of their belief system before passing; if they regard what they did as a sin against God, then they may indeed suffer great anguish and

28

shame; but worst of all would be the knowledge that they had terminated a plan which might have proved a great step forward in their spiritual progression. For perhaps their suffering was preparing them for a wonderful future of service to others, which would, in time, have proved richly fulfilling.

There are of course many reasons for suicide, such as: being unable to bear continued physical pain caused by accident, illness, disease or torture. Or through suppression in certain countries, offering little hope of what seems a worthwhile existence. Then, and to some extent in all cases, there is mental anguish and instability, despair, despondency and over-bearing depression, a feeling of being unloved, of no value, and not cared for, all of which can lead to suicide.

As I have said, all who commit suicide are met whenever possible, but sometimes it is not immediately possible for them to be met, not because those in the spirit world do not love and want to help them, for it is always the case that they do; but on certain occasions individuals who pass unnaturally, whether a suicidal act or any other form of passing, will not accept or believe that they have actually passed, for their 'new' spiritual body is identical to their former earthly body, and feels as tangible to them, as our bodies feel to us upon earth. Many who commit suicide of course do not truly mean to succeed, and after passing, through desire, remain attached to the earth plane; they might also be held close to earth by their mental and emotional state and ties, perhaps desiring to remain near to another individual upon earth, or within a particular area or building to which they feel an attraction. Indeed the state of mind, and pre-conceived ideas contained within the mind, can be of vital importance: if one expects to be alone, at rest, awaiting the day of resurrection at the last trumpet, then they are likely to create the conditions of this 'reality' for themselves. Knowledge, the truth that a beautiful spirit world full of life and happiness exists, and awaits us all, is therefore of great importance, and will save countless numbers from needlessly inflicting a self-made purgatory upon themselves.

Additionally, there is another reason for a suicide victim becoming what is known as 'earthbound', and this is because the unexpected passing does not allow for the dissolution of their etheric body. For in a natural or expected passing the etheric body, which helps to sustain and energise the physical body, slowly dissolves, and its link with the physical body and the subsequent energy it provides, is reduced until a natural passing occurs, freeing the soul and spirit to return to the spirit world. But, if the passing is unnatural, unexpected and sudden, then the connection of the spirit with the etheric body can hold them back, until their etheric body dissolves; and this has to happen before they can permanently move on, because the etheric body vibrates at a frequency close to the earth vibration, and is therefore unable to move into the spirit world; because: the various levels of the spirit world vibrate at a range of much higher frequencies; and the lower etheric cannot penetrate the higher spiritual.

Although the dissolution of the etheric body might take but a short time, to a suicide victim, who is already in an emotionally disturbed state, added to the shock of finding themselves still alive and feeling lost, their new circumstances can, for a time, prove too overwhelming for them to face, and this can cause them to withdraw from any possible communication with their loved ones in the spirit world. They may also be fearful of loved ones they know to have passed, in much the same way in which many would be scared of one they consider a ghost, and their fear and confused state of mind (perhaps thinking they are hallucinating or having a bad dream) can make it difficult for help from the spirit world to directly reach them. For the fear must first be reduced: and it is at this time when the prayers of those upon earth can be of the greatest benefit, for all prayers will help. The prayer for the victim should ask for them to be guided, and for them to move toward the light, sending love, and the thoughts and energy within the prayer will help them. As those of us upon earth, being at a similar vibratory level to the victim, and therefore in a sense closer to them, are often in a better position to give this initial help.

Such prayers carry a vibration of love, and even if the victim is not able to initially recognise the thoughts being directed toward them, such energy and goodwill contained can enter their thoughts via their subconscious mind, and in time bring relief and greater peace of mind, allowing guides and helpers to draw close, and to help the unfortunate victim. Without such help the victim may remain earthbound for sometime, but for how long it is impossible to say, for their mind will still be active, and when they are ready and willing to accept and receive help, it will arrive, for always there are those more advanced souls awaiting the opportunity to be of service to such a 'lost' soul, and when such a soul is ready, they will guide them to their next sphere of life.

5. AT WHAT POINT DOES LIFE BEGIN & WHAT ARE THE CONSEQUENCES OF ABORTION?

Life upon earth in physical form begins at conception (although the spirit may spend most of their time in the spirit world); and if the spirit who intends to use the newly forming physical body has lived in human form before, and is therefore to reincarnate they, with the help of angels, will have played their own part in the forming of their physical body-to-be. They will have helped by forming an etheric body around the developing embryo, and this forms a connection which interpenetrates with the physical body. This could be likened to a spirit umbilical cord, linking the spirit to the physical body; it is a link which will not be broken until 'death' occurs. If the birth is to be one of a new-soul, a spirit who has never before experienced individualised consciousness, at least not in human form, then all necessary help will be given by the particular angels who are masters of human form creation.

Upon earth, abortion is mainly viewed in two different ways: one arguing that to terminate a pregnancy is against the will of God, and therefore similar to murder; the other arguing it is the mother's body which bears the strain, and she who will face the years of nurturing her child, and therefore it is her right to choose whether to proceed.

The first point to make clear is that no spirit, and the supreme architect we call God, will not sit in judgment upon any mother or father who decide, for whatever personal reason, to terminate a pregnancy, and there will certainly be no punishment awaiting them. Indeed, I have heard it said that on occasions a would-be reincarnating spirit may choose to terminate their link before their would-be physical body is fully formed, causing a miscarriage; although I'm sure there would generally be a good reason for a plan to change at a late stage.

When an abortion is performed the spirit who would have incarnated will of course be forced to withdraw, but they will suffer no physical pain; although they might be frustrated, disappointed and upset. For perhaps on a higher level of consciousness, away from the confusion we can all fall victim to upon earth, the mother (and father) may not have wished to terminate her pregnancy, and had been planning to provide a physical body and home for a spirit friend as her child. The spirit might at a later stage make further attempts to fulfil the plan with the same mother, but if unsuccessful might agree to another plan, and eventually incarnate through someone else. While a new to human form soul, having been aborted from the physical world, would be forced to continue their long spiritual climb in the spirit world, where, as mentioned in answer number 3, they would grow and be well cared for.

It would certainly be advisable for any parent, or would-be parent, to consider the question of whether to have an abortion from a spiritual perspective before making a final decision; although the decision is their own to make. For plans made in the spirit world for intended incarnations are not decided by mere whim; they are carefully considered for all parties involved, not just the child, and can be far reaching in complexity. We need only think of the many hundreds of different people we meet from childhood and throughout life, to consider how delicate the planning can be, all of which spirit masters somehow weigh in the life-plan, which is agreed before birth; and all such plans are designed to give valued and necessary experiences for spiritual growth.

An abortion will therefore interfere with plans made on a higher level of consciousness, perhaps denying (albeit temporarily) many people experiences which would have unfolded during the intended life-span of the spirit who was to incarnate. This does not mean necessary experiences will be lost forever, for many plans are developed and adjusted as life progresses, but it does delay and complicate the progression and spiritual development of those involved. Since the true purpose of life is spiritual growth: any action which hinders and delays this will, with hindsight gained upon passing, be something which will be of regret, but the opportunity to gain any necessary experience will present itself again, where necessary--in a future incarnation.

6. DO ANIMALS SURVIVE 'DEATH'?

All life is continuous, so all who have lost a pet with whom they built a bond of love will, upon their own passing, find that the pet has survived 'death'. In the meantime he or she will have been cared for and looked after either by one of their friends or relatives who recognised their mutual love, or by one of the many in the spirit world who engage themselves in the task of caring for such animals. Indeed this is a service which true animal lovers could engage themselves in when they pass. Pets, as all who love them know, are very often better than people at returning and reciprocating love, and perhaps more appropriately might be called companions, and it is this mutual love which enables pets to wait for their former owners.

Every aspect of the spirit world is built upon happiness and love, with no hunger, thirst, cold or fear, the passage of earth time is not noticed; memories therefore stay fresh in the mind of any pet, and when the one they love eventually passes to the spirit world, no matter how many years this may take, the pet will greet them with love as though they were apart for just a short while. Additionally, the pet might very well be brought to visit those they love upon earth, indeed many people have reported seeing, hearing and feeling a departed pet.

Animals have a higher self, a group consciousness or soul, the experiences of one animal of a particular group enabling the whole group to learn; and in this way they help each other in their progression. Those animals who do not have a relationship of individual love with people, such as wild or herd animals, return to merge with their group; which is forever progressing and incarnating new life upon earth. Although, even in the wild, some animals learn and progress quicker than others, and such animals may develop to become group leaders, and in turn help and teach others of their group; ensuring that progression is always naturally in operation.

We should all give more love and kindness to animals, as they are on an evolutionary pathway just as all of creation is; and I believe that in time mankind will develop to the degree that the eating of, and experimentation upon, all animals will cease; and that to future generations of mankind, such acts, will seem just as barbaric and primitive as cannibalism and human sacrifices today seem to us.

Additionally, and worthy of consideration, is the fact that during our spiritual evolution we all change form many times. Therefore, during our long existence we might have all passed through stages of development when we might have incarnated in the form of one or more animal, although not necessarily upon this planet. Therefore, it is also quite possible that a beloved cat, dog, or other developed animal, might be housing the spirit of one who will eventually reach a sufficient level of consciousness, or self-awareness, so that at some point in their near future it will prove possible for them to incarnate in human form.

Chapter Two

PERSONAL & PHILOSOPHICAL

Questions 7-12

==

7. IF WE HAVE MARRIED TWICE, DO WE HAVE TO CHOOSE BETWEEN OUR FORMER PARTNERS AFTER 'DEATH'?

We are told by spirit communicators that life in the spirit world is rather different from life upon the earth; there are still 'rules', things we can do and things we cannot do; but these 'rules' are known as universal or natural laws, and are not man-made rules, they are God's laws in operation.

Upon earth, over the centuries many ideas of how life should be organised, controlled and ruled have been instigated; but all of these ideas are man-made, and in most cases, including marriage, they have no bearing, or consequence in the spirit world.

Life in the spirit world is in harmonious accord with the natural laws of God, and with regard to relationships, subject to natural attractions: which are much clearer than their counterpart upon earth, where our attractions can be of a more superficial nature. If we have had two or twenty two marriage partners it would not be of importance to anyone progressed in the spirit world; and each of us is free to be with whichever partner we choose, provided our attraction and desire is reciprocated. Or, if we so choose, we do not have to be with either or any partner, for each of us is a free spirit and, as such: we have total freedom of choice.

Marriage, as an institution, does not exist in the spirit world; upon earth it can sometimes tie us into situations and circumstances which may not necessarily be good for us. It is of course good to show loyalty to a partner, as it would be to any friend, especially in a marriage where children are involved; but what we really need upon earth is greater honesty, spoken communication, and a more mutually flexible loyalty, allowing each of us the opportunity to expand and grow. For even with so-called equality too many marriages are one-sided, with the man dominating, and in many ways taking far more than 50%, which, quite rightly, can cause many females to feel used. I am not advocating more promiscuity, in fact the whole subject is given far too much credence and publicity; which is itself one of the causes of unrest, and in this respect the media and their materialistic methods of selling have a lot to answer for. What is needed is more flexibility and freedom to progress in the way our spirit directs, with spiritual virtues taking a more prominent role in our lives. Denying expression can cause a great deal of stress, and this can lead to health problems, and to the severance of what might have otherwise been a happy worthwhile partnership.

Life in the spirit world leaves each of us free from the restraints and commitments of incarnation, and allows full expression in whichever way we choose to express ourselves. If this happens to be as a group of two or more this is entirely a decision for each of those concerned to make. Jealousy should not exist between former partners upon earth, for in the spirit world we are in a position to understand that life holds far more riches than the attention one single individual can possibly give;

38

although it is of course perfectly all right to have individual attention if both desire it.

During life in the spirit world, by choice, the time may come when partners who have been happy together for a great length of time will part, even if temporarily, for perhaps one or both might desire a pursuit different to the other. When, and if, such a time should come, each will be ready to accept the separation, understanding that in a mere thought they can be together again; it is all up to those concerned, love in the spirit world allowing for the expression and freedom each of us will gladly give to the other. Trying to hold-on to someone who does not desire it, is not a true expression of love, to express love we must be willing to give, and to allow the same freedom to others we would wish for ourselves.

Therefore, if we have had more than one partner upon earth, and we feel unsure where we will belong, we should not worry, for our heart will choose, as will the heart of each former partner. If we love two, then who knows, we might form a small group, for there are no rules to deny love its freedom of expression.

8. WHY ARE WE BORN?

We are all born in order to learn lessons, through experiences and, in this way, we progress as more enlightened spiritual beings. With each physical lifetime teaching us a little more, until finally we reach the level where we no longer need to return to earth; although, even at this stage of attainment, we might still choose to be born, in order to serve as a teacher, or a healer, for the guidance and benefit of others.

For the vast majority of us our current incarnation is unlikely to be our first in human form, and it would not have been forced upon us; it would have been arranged with our co-operation and agreement and, at some time before birth, we would have been asked, along with others with whom we were to share certain experiences, whether we were willing to undertake a certain plan, like a blueprint for life. This being designed in order for us to experience lessons desirable for our personal spiritual progression; although there is no guarantee the desired lessons will unfold as planned, since from the very moment of birth, each of us has had free-will and the choice of if, when, and how we progress will have been our decision, our personal responsibility.

During physical life, once the spiritual value of one lesson has been learned, another lesson inevitably presents itself; one of the lessons is to learn to establish a balance between the spiritual and the physical, by living and learning lessons: often not recognisable by our own perception of lessons; then gradually, over the passage of time and through many lifetimes, we gradually become finer and wiser spiritual beings.

Through our many physical lifetimes we are able to experience a variety of situations and outcomes, to learn by our inter-actions with others, and although it is nearly impossible to identify individual lessons we might be here to experience and learn from, on a broad scale: lessons of universal love, kindness, compassion, peace and understanding are all part of the spiritual virtues which are eventually to be mastered. Our teachers have learned to show a great deal of patience, and this too is something which might well take us many attempts to master.

So the true broader purpose of life is to help ourselves and others to grow spiritually, as finer spirit beings, and therefore evolve closer to God. This does not mean life should not be enjoyed, for we should always try to live in happiness and harmony; if we live by the motto that we will only ever do unto others that which we would have done to ourselves, life will prove much simpler, more rewarding, and less stressful.

Upon the conclusion of our current incarnations we will return to the spirit world, where we will review our efforts during this lifetime; we will then be in a much better position to judge whether we responded to our lessons in the appropriate manner. We will also be able to see and understand why some may have needed repeating several times, which lessons we gained from and, which ones might, in a future incarnation, need further attempts to master.

9. DOES IT MATTER HOW WE LIVE OUR LIFE, SINCE WE WILL SURVIVE ANYWAY?

How we live our lives is of great importance, not only does it have an effect upon our present day to day circumstances, but it can also influence future incarnations, as well as life in one of the many realms of the spirit world. We should all strive to live in harmony with the yearnings of our own spirit, while duly respecting others; to do so: we should use our inner feelings from the heart, or our intuition, and to allow these feelings to be our guide.

We must recognise that the law of karma, or cause and effect, is forever in operation; guaranteeing that "as we sow, so shall we reap" or to put it another way "an eye for an eye", which although misused by mankind as permission to take revenge and pass judgment upon others, simply means that through the law of karma whatever we do in this life: will have repercussions which will rebound to or against us by way of natural law, perhaps later in this life, perhaps in a future incarnation. So we should all take care, for eventually the consequences of our actions can do no other than take effect upon us. If we are sensible we will strive to live in harmony and, if we do slip up on occasions: try to put things right as soon as possible, and thus avoid the consequences of undesired karma.

This can often be achieved by a simple apology if we have upset someone; for even if we are not technically in the wrong, it still never hurts to say sorry for any upset accidentally caused. In this way we can also help the other person to release their tensions and, be sowing good seeds for our own future.

How we have lived life will indeed be of great importance to us when we return to the spirit world, for we will then be able to judge whether we have made any spiritual progression; and if we find we have ignored all the opportunities we have had to progress, we will be very sorry indeed; while if we have responded to and progressed from the opportunities we have had, we will of course be highly delighted.

It is not necessary for us to worry over every action we take in life, and certainly no spirit world guide would wish us to live in fear, for as long as the knowledge of our true nature is within, with greater spiritual understanding, we should naturally become more tolerant of others, and better able to understand ourselves; when necessary we will then be able to remind ourselves of our true eternal spiritual nature, and be in a position to allow our spirit within to guide us.

Personal responsibility must always be borne in mind, if we know something is not right, even at a deep level, and continue to ignore our inner knowing, we will reap the consequences of undesired karma. For example: those who preach orthodox religious dogma: denying the truth of communication from those in the spirit world, and the possible beneficial effects of Spiritual healing, if at any level of understanding they know their teachings to be incorrect, they will have to pay the price; and their karma for a future incarnation might very well involve them having to personally teach the truth to all whom they have misled. The only 'remission' they might be lucky enough to receive, is when the individuals they misled, have in the meantime, learned the truth.

Ultimately, what happens to us on the outside, the precise detail of our physical life, is not of great importance. It is our reactions and responses to the experiences of life which determine our spiritual growth, and it is this which is of importance to us. The consequences of which will also be reflected in future incarnations, for what we sow or earn in our current incarnation will have an influence upon our next one; with perhaps, depending upon individual circumstances, even our next physical body bearing the consequences of the karma we have sown; so it is always beneficial to live harmoniously, in every aspect of life.

10. IS THERE ANYTHING TO BE GAINED BY THE UNDERSTANDING OF SURVIVAL AFTER 'DEATH', & BY THE STUDY OF SPIRITUAL TEACHINGS?

By understanding the factual truth of survival after 'death', and the knowledge which spiritual teachings bring of eternal life and natural laws, we should feel more encouraged to question every action of our own lives; and thus potentially enhance our spiritual growth and progression. For as we judge ourselves and our motives in all we say or do, with the realisation that none of us can escape the consequences of our thoughts, words and deeds, we have the opportunity, and therefore should, become more spiritually enlightened beings.

Thus, understanding allows us the chance to make great advances in our spiritual progression, while also of course encouraging us to be more reasonable in our actions, for we realise that whatever we think, say or do, will ultimately be revealed; with good and kindly thoughts, words and deeds, reaping rewards either in this life, our spirit world life, or in a future incarnation.

This greater understanding of natural laws should always be considered a blessing, for it is always better to have knowledge than to be ignorant; it should never be considered a burden, with every action being weighed against us, for we all make mistakes, poor judgements, and take wrong actions, if we were perfect we would not need to be here. Although, it should help us to be more tolerant of others, and more able to correct our own mistakes, and by so doing, whether by word or deed, we can help ourselves in this life, and in our life to come. As this understanding becomes more deeply rooted in our mind, we should, in time, and with practice, find that our actions spontaneously take this reality into account, and when this happens, we are really making spiritual progress.

The study of spiritual teachings should enhance and expand our understanding, bringing to us all the more wisdom and reason for living life with a spiritual outlook; study---while supplying answers---will at the same time create more questions, as spiritual awakening brings the desire for more knowledge, truth and wisdom. We in the Western world have been starved of truth in our upbringing, the truth of the television news only tells part of the truth, mainly the negative side; with spiritual knowledge we can understand the positive, starting with the fact that we, and everyone else in the world is immortal, and that nobody has, or ever will, truly die. By absorbing spiritual teachings we therefore become more aware of our true purpose for living, and this awareness allows us to direct our lives in accordance with natural laws, reaping greater rewards, and progressing much further than might be possible for those who unfortunately, or through lack of desire, are without understanding.

11. IS EVERY ACTION OF LIFE PLANNED, OR CAN FREE-WILL CHANGE WHAT WOULD OTHERWISE BE OUR DESTINY?

We are born with a life plan, a blueprint, which we agreed to on a higher level before birth, with even those souls who are new to individualised consciousness in human form considered in the complex planning undertaken by highly evolved souls who, by some, are considered archangels, and called *Lords of Karma*.₁ Our lives are planned to give the greatest opportunity for spiritual growth; with experiences and lessons we need for the further progression of our spirit. Obviously it is a plan we should wish to co-operate with, as this will, in the long term, give us the greatest progress; however, since while we are on earth we do not remember the plan, it is one we can inadvertently stray from.

Free-will: can at times cause havoc and completely ruin our plans, destroying what might have otherwise been our destiny;

but since our plan is for certain experiences and lessons which enable us to grow and progress spiritually, many of the physical considerations can be adjusted and altered, and still allow for our experiences and lessons to unfold. So often the pathway we take in life will redirect us back onto a suitable route to complete our planned spiritual destiny; which is to learn through experiences the lessons we came to undertake, with ultimately the precise physical detail being of little relevance (in the long term--this does not mean we should ignore our physical well-being).

Sometimes the re-direction is a result of our higher consciousness: being sufficiently able to make us rethink our life; while at other times it is the prompting of our guides and helpers, directing us onto a similar pathway, one which will lead us to fulfil our life plan. Prompting usually filters through from the subconscious mind in the form of an intuitive feeling, or our conscience, telling us if a certain pathway is the right one; but of course all possible prompting will not help some people, especially those who have learned to crave and covet the physical pleasures of life, and it is most likely that they will not successfully experience all they wished and planned for on a higher level before birth. So when they return to the spirit world they will have regrets, and through need, may on a future occasion choose to try once more to experience the lessons which they should have completed in their current incarnation.

Probably the only way for us to attempt co-operation: is to follow the intuition of our heart, to let love, compassion and one-ship with all others upon this planet be our guiding light in all dealings. In other words, we need to develop greater universal and unconditional love for all life, for it is of little value to love family and friends while ignoring those we do not personally know, for in reality all are part of the one God. I do not think any of us will go too far astray if we manage to follow this simple philosophy; but we will never truly know, until we return to the spirit world, all we can do is our best, and pray that everything for us is unfolding as it should.

12. ARE WE JUDGED UPON 'DEATH', AND IF SO BY WHOM?

Upon 'death' the only judge we have is ourselves. Many spirit world people have reported being shown a replay of their entire life in what seemed to them a matter of seconds or minutes, with their good and bad points highlighted. But all have reported that it was themselves who acted as judge or assessor, with feelings of happiness and delight accompanying their good and better moments, while sadness overcame many when they reviewed moments of regret.

We should therefore not fear any great day of judgment with entry into heaven or hell the reward or sentence; but at the same time we should consider that as our own judge we are likely to be more critical of ourselves than we would be of another. I would therefore advise most strongly against us ignoring our own shortcomings, and assuming we will simply forgive ourselves, for when we review the facts with spiritual hindsight this simply will not happen. Natural laws are also in operation, and our efforts and therefore progression in this life will determine our place in the spirit world, the responsibility is most certainly our own.

Like attracts like, and the sphere we progress to is going to be filled with people on a similar spiritual par to ourselves; so if anyone thinks this sounds rather disheartening, they still have time to change their ways and perhaps progress a little higher. But whatever is undertaken to achieve this: must come from the heart, although sometimes through continued practice and effort it is possible to retrain ourselves into new and better habits, which become a way of life. By showing compassion, friendship and care for all others we can begin the process; and indeed often simple friendliness has become overlooked in this commercial, stressful world. If we but make the effort to show concern for others, polite friendship, kindness and compassion, we soon realise this is by far the best and most rewarding way to live, and I'm sure the majority of us have already put these principles into practise, but it never hurts to be reminded.

Chapter Three

SUFFERING

Questions 13-18

==

13. IF GOD IS ALL SEEING AND ALL KNOWING, WHY IS SO MUCH SUFFERING PERMITTED IN THE WORLD?

The omnipresent consciousness we call God does not limit our spiritual growth by decreeing which lessons are available to us, allowing us the pleasure of one, while shielding us from another because it is painful; if this was so we would not develop with a complete or balanced understanding, and our spiritual progression and attainment would be restricted. God has given us free-will, and personal responsibility, for all of our thoughts, words and deeds, and this allows each of us the choice of how, when and where we undertake to experience the many and varied lessons of life; including, if we so choose, suffering. While suffering can also be caused by our own, or the actions of others, and might not be a pre-planned or even a desirable lesson.

When we see the suffering that some souls experience it is only natural that our response should be one of regret, compassion and sympathy; we are of course unable to see why anyone might, if indeed they have, chosen a particular learning experience, nor can we comprehend the full value they may reap from the lesson. All such deliberate decisions being undertaken upon that higher level of consciousness before birth, when each of us is fully aware of their value. Such lessons indeed help the spiritual growth and development of an individual, producing a deeper understanding of suffering and the response of compassion, therefore those who experience suffering are far better equipped to help others who suffer. As already stated, suffering can also be caused by inappropriate actions, but it is not the responsibility of God to stop these, indeed this too is another lesson for us and others, and sometimes for mankind as a whole.

Suffering is of course a transient experience, and one which can add to our understanding, allowing us to grow in knowledge; this may sound harsh and perhaps unfeeling, and we might well consider those who through no fault of their own suffer greatly, such as those forced through accident or disease to live their life in a wheelchair. But as unfeeling as it may indeed appear to sound, there might be reasons: lessons being learned, and the lessons can also be shared by those who might be confronted with the responsibility of caring for the victims; for sometimes a brave soul might volunteer to come as a victim to help teach those around them.

God is all seeing and all knowing because we are all aspects of God, therefore whatever we do is instantaneously known to God; if we suffer unfairly, through no fault of our own (which can happen), this is also known, and we will receive some form of compensation, perhaps at a later stage in our current incarnation, perhaps when we return to the spirit world, and perhaps in a future incarnation; for in time everything will balance fairly, and this must be so, for God's infallible natural laws are forever in operation.

It is therefore not the responsibility of God to stop or prevent suffering, we, as eternal spiritual beings have to learn and progress to the degree where we no longer create, through our thoughts, words and deeds, the suffering of mankind, the responsibility is our own.

14. WHY ARE SOME PEOPLE BORN WITH PHYSICAL OR MENTAL HANDICAPS?

There could be several reasons why someone might be born into a physical body which is imperfect in some way. One possible reason, as mentioned in the previous answer, is that such a life was chosen on a higher level of consciousness before birth, so the spirit could experience and learn from the difficulties that such an incarnation brings.

Suffering teaches compassion, especially toward those who experience the same form of suffering; therefore if an individual suffers with their own back, they are very aware and understanding of another who suffers with a back problem; while someone who has multiple sclerosis understands the frustrations of a fellow multiple sclerosis sufferer; and those with a heart problem understand the limitations of a fellow heart sufferer.

We can all feel compassion and sympathy for others who suffer, in any form (mind, body or spirit), but to fully understand and appreciate we often need to have experience of a similar problem for ourselves. So it is likely that some, especially those born with a handicap, chose, while on a higher level of consciousness, to experience the frustrations, limitations, pain and anguish they undergo upon earth.

But I would add: this does not mean we should treat sufferers with any less compassion and sympathy; in one way we should treat them with more, for if they did choose such an incarnation

51

they have been very brave, and for such an act of bravery, and subsequent life, they not only deserve our compassion and sympathy, but also our admiration and respect.

I also do not believe everyone can be neatly fitted into the category of 'born to suffer' an experience predetermined before birth; accidents, mistakes and errors do occur, and it is mankind's free-will which is often to blame, for collective free-will can and does have an effect upon us all, with every action producing a reaction, a cause and effect. Therefore the many wrong actions undertaken by mankind during recent decades are producing effects, (example: atmospheric pollution---causing asthma) which all too often cause innocent victims to suffer. This is one of the reasons why it is so important for spiritual knowledge: particularly karma, the law of cause and effect, to be understood by all mankind.

15. WHY DO SOME PEOPLE HAVE AN EASIER LIFE THAN OTHERS?

Before birth we co-operate with spiritual masters to agree a life plan; the precision this extends to is quite detailed, and includes knowledge of who our parents are going to be, and the name we are to be called by, with even the exact moment of our birth having been calculated to attract certain astrological influences (vibrations). But more importantly our plan is for certain lessons, pertaining to our needs, to be undertaken for the benefit of our own (and possibly others) spiritual growth and progression. For this purpose it is not always, and in fact rarely desirable, to incarnate into what we might, while using our physical senses, consider an idyllic life-style.

So for all, with the exception of 'new' human souls, who are initially helped by advanced souls, everything should have started out as we planned. If we think of ourselves as actors who have been cast to play the part most suitable for us at this particular stage of our acting career in: "a life upon earth", for some a simple part as an average person is ideal, while others are just right for the star role as hero or martyr, this time around we play one part, and perhaps next time a completely different role. All, in the grand scheme of things, will eventually balance fairly, and we will have played all the parts necessary to have completed a full and comprehensive program of learning; then perhaps we can take on the role of the director.

It is often considered that those born into a family with more financial wealth are luckier; but just because they have more money does not necessarily mean they have an easier life (when viewed from the perspective of spiritual lessons); it is often just as difficult, albeit in ways differing from the problems of those who are financially poor. For instance, someone who inherits a family business might suddenly find themselves shouldering the responsibility of continued prosperity, so that the loyal staff might continue to be employed and paid. Their decisions might affect the livelihood and well-being of many people, and while some might take such responsibility lightly, someone with sensitivity and compassion might feel under great pressure.

While a native South American Indian: born to a life in the jungle, has no money, and this never worries him, he is more concerned with food and shelter. Those of us born in the so-called civilised world, with adequate food and shelter, so often create unnecessary worries for ourselves, over possessions which, in truth: we often do not need. For so often our worries concern luxuries, about which we become jealous and envious

53

of those with more luxuries than ourselves; wasting our time in a quest for what, one minute after our 'death', will prove meaningless to us.

We would therefore be wise not to concern ourselves with how and why some people may seem to have an easier life; it could also be borne in mind that more hardship can bring more scope for learning, and therefore greater possibilities of spiritual growth and progression. Remembering that in eternity all will eventually balance fairly and, that it is only what we have spiritually gained from this life which is truly worth possessing and, of course, all we can ultimately take with us.

16. WHAT CAN BE SAID TO COMFORT THE BEREAVED?

It is very difficult to know exactly what to say to someone who, because of the bereavement of a loved one, is suffering emotionally. For each passing is personal to those remaining, and none of us are exactly alike, so will react and respond in a different way.

Whatever is said must therefore be with great care and tenderness, gently expressing love and concern for their feelings, and slowly introducing the truth, as understood, to them. If they already have awareness and knowledge of spiritual teachings they will, hopefully, be in a better position to come to terms with their loss. But just because they have spiritual understanding does not necessarily make the loss easy to bear, as they will miss and grieve the loss of the physical presence of the loved one.

Those with knowledge can slowly and gently be reminded of it, and be encouraged to consider how their loved one will now be in a place of beauty and harmony, of how they are very likely watching and wondering what all the fuss is about; since they will undoubtedly be perfectly happy in their new life.

If the one who is in need of comfort does not have any spiritual knowledge, the same truth can slowly be introduced to them; and, as they respond and are ready, they can gradually be given more information, bringing more comfort, understanding, and peace of mind.

The first point which will probably be of concern to them is whether their departed loved one is still truly alive, and then whether they are all right and happy in their new life and world. The truth of life after 'death' can therefore be explained: that nobody ever truly dies; that if their loved one suffered any pain they will now be free of all such suffering, and if they had any physical problems or handicaps these will have disappeared. It can also be explained that the body they will now be using, their spiritual body, is a perfect one, full of health, vigour and strength. That where they will now live there is no hunger or thirst, and that there are no cold winters. Also, that they will have no reason for sadness; for they are now in a world where they can see and understand the true nature of life. They no longer have anything to worry or cause them fear; for their new quality of life will be far superior to life on earth, in a perfect, friendly, harmonious, loving land of pure delight.

They can further be told that the loved one would have been met by their relatives and friends in the spirit world; and that if the loved one had previously mourned the passing of another, they would now be reunited. Furthermore, if they had loved a pet animal, who passed before them, they can be told how the animals survive, and of how they would also have been waiting for them.

They can also be told the loved one will be able to visit them, and will be much happier to see them continuing with their life in a cheerful manner; for if they visit and see them sad it might sadden them; although the loved one is now in a world where the sadness of earth need not disturb them; for they are now in a world in which they can express themselves in all manner of ways, with no financial or other restrictions which might have prevented such expression upon earth.

They can also be told what should really be considered good news, that since we are all here to learn lessons, the loved one had more than likely completed all of theirs; and their spirit was therefore free, and happy to return to our true home, heaven, the spirit world.

17. IS IT RIGHT THAT SO MANY ANIMALS SUFFER AT THE HANDS OF MANKIND & WOULD VEGETARIANISM BE A WORTHY PURSUIT?

This question needs to consider a whole range of issues, from general treatment of pets and working animals, in relation to hunting and so called "blood-sports", whether experimentation and vivisection of animals can be justified and, importantly, whether animals should be eaten.

The first point to make absolutely and categorically clear is that all animals, as with all life forms, are on their own evolutionary pathway of spiritual progression. I have heard people who might consider themselves advanced upon their own pathway of spiritual progression say something like 'mankind has dominion over animals' as they prepare to eat a meal; and I'll deal with the vegetarian aspect shortly. But first I must make it clear that if mankind has any dominion over animals it is purely as a spiritual teacher, with the responsibility for helping them along their own spiritual pathways of progression, we do not own them body, mind and spirit, and they were certainly not put upon this planet for us to do with as we please, and generally abuse.

Pets should be treated with love and respect, fed sensibly, generally made to feel at home, and as members of the household. Those who are unable to take proper care of pets, or unable to devote them sufficient time for their needs, should not have one, it is as simple as that. A pet cannot be treated as a living convenience, there when the human desires to bother with them, they have feelings and emotions, and often become ill if not given the love and companionship they need, regardless of how well fed they might be. Working animals, such as farm and race horses are very much the same; if cared for and in good health they enjoy their work, or racing, provided it is without punishment. They also enjoy being groomed and having human contact, someone taking interest in them, if neglected they become depressed just the same as humans do.

The hunting of animals, especially in what are disgustingly called "blood-sports" is a total abomination to the human spirit. When ancient races such as the native American Indians hunted, it was purely out of necessity for food and material for clothing, respect was shown to the animals, as it was given to all of nature. A prayer was offered-up before the hunt commenced, and the spirit of the animal whose lot it was to be killed to feed the tribe was informed, through prayer, of the reason for its physical demise, and how it was not done out of meaningless malice or for pleasure, but through necessity. These days people have no reason to hunt animals for food or for material for clothing, and those who do so for pleasure, especially when cruelty is involved: by terrifying the poor animal over miles of chase, are truly indulging in a barbaric pastime fit only for the lowest upon the spiritual ladder of evolution. "Blood-sports" are a pastime which should be banned in all countries which call themselves civilised. There is no excuse to justify such behaviour; the most common excuse offered by those who practice such as fox and stag hunting is: that their actions are necessary to cull certain animals; what an insult to the human spirit. If over-population (in 'our' opinion), means that some animals should be culled (killed!), to reduce their numbers, a situation which only ever arises because of mankind's interference with nature, it should be done in the most humane manner possible, with due apologies offered to the spirits of the creatures killed.

Over the centuries mankind has always striven to find cures for the multitude of ailments suffered. The most successful remedies have always been natural, from nature, from plant, flower, herb, and tree. Only more recently are we finding (or rediscovering) other alternatives, such as vibrational treatments, and the re-emergence of Spiritual healing. These treatments can prove beneficial without causing the destruction of animals, or any suffering to another life-form; and are in harmony with the human spirit. Experimentation and vivisection of animals to find cures and answers to human ailments can never be a justifiable method of gaining knowledge. In the vast majority of cases the efforts are totally without result, and succeed only in bringing suffering and death to countless numbers of innocent animals who look to humankind (human-unkind) for guidance, only to be rewarded with a pitiless destruction in the most degrading manner and circumstances imaginable. Such insulting treatment of animals should cease immediately, for we are doing ourselves no good whatsoever by such non-spiritual behaviour.

Some might argue that certain medicines and cures have been found as a result of such experimentation; but can these results truly justify the suffering of the innocent? By my understanding of spiritual laws, God's natural laws of the universe and nature, we can only reap according to how we sow. Therefore, if we abuse animals (or any other creature, each other, or the earth planet) we are sowing very poor seeds, and will have to pay the karmic price for our actions, for we all know, however hard some might try to deny it, or justify such misdeeds, that such mistreatment of animals is wrong; and, as we all become more aware of karma, the spiritual law of cause and effect, and its consequences, the more we will realise how demeaning to the spirit such behaviour is.

Another point I would like readers to consider, is that the karma, which inevitably (in some form) must be created by our actions, might very well manifest as disease; which further makes a mockery of trying to find remedies through such deplorable and inhumane deeds. In other words, such actions are themselves likely to be one of the causes of world-wide disease, for as we give out, or send forth vibrations of death, destruction, pain and misery, so the vibrations in the circle of life return to us in full measure, being the inescapable consequences of cause and effect (karma).

Finally we come to the question of whether vegetarianism would be a worthy pursuit. I have personally put this question to a spirit guide, as well as hearing others do likewise. The answer is really twofold: from the point of view (which I too share) of an ideal to aim for, it is indeed a worthy one, and with the passage of the decades I believe a great many people will change their diets. Partially this will occur through a desire to be healthier, but also it will be through spiritual awakening, when greater and still greater numbers of the human race accept their true status as eternal spiritual beings, and at the same time recognise the fact animals are, like themselves, spiritual beings.

But as I said, the answer is twofold: for I have been told that certain animals, as a group, at some point in history: volunteered to incarnate with the knowledge that they would be used by humans as a food source. This of course does not mean it will be their destiny for all eternity, and they will eventually reap the benefits of their remarkable sacrifice. Once more: we can return to the concern for the treatment of such animals, if their lives (until mankind learns better) are destined to be cut short to help mankind continue their needless consumption of animal flesh, in the manner they have grown accustomed, it is only fitting that their shortened lives should be reasonably pleasant ones, without cruelty, without suffering, and without needless fear. If not, the consequences reaped by the sowing of mankind will be the consumption of animal flesh which might well carry an unhealthy vibration, and once more karma will seek balance through necessary retribution, which inevitably must be exacted through the outworking of natural laws.

For those who do decide to change their eating habits, the recommendation I heard the spirit guides suggest: is to change gradually, perhaps over a period of a month or two, for the bodies of many people have grown accustomed to the eating of animal fats, and this can also be genetically inherited in the genes, and, for some, a sudden change in diet could cause mild withdrawal symptoms, perhaps resulting in a feeling of lightheadedness. The change of diet can be supplemented by vitamins and minerals, which can be added to the diet to ensure an adequately healthy and balanced intact is maintained, particularly during the change-over period. Although, with just a little study it soon becomes apparent: that all the necessary intake of protein and nutrients is readily available, without us ever needing to destroy and consume a single animal, let alone the millions upon millions of animals that are bred, often to spend their entire lives in miserable conditions, before being terrified during their final moments in the slaughter houses (or death camps) before being destroyed.

Indeed, in a book called *The New Why You Don't Need Meat* by Peter Cox, there is a table which clearly shows that the human body is designed as Vegetarian, and not as a flesh eater.[1] For human beings and vegetarian animals have hands (or hoofs), flat teeth, long intestines to fully digest nutrients in plant foods, we sweat to cool our bodies, sip water, obtain vitamin C solely from our diet, and a number of other vegetarian factors; while animals which are flesh eaters have claws (not hands or hoofs), sharp teeth, short intestines to rapidly excrete putrefying flesh, they pant to cool their bodies, lap water, and internally manufacture vitamin C, plus numerous other differences to human beings and vegetarian animals.

Have we always eaten animal flesh? Many people mistakenly believe so, but in the same book this point is answered thus:[2]

"Scientific evidence suggests that our ancestors probably originated in the East African Rift Valley, which is a dry and desolate place today, but would have been very different 2-4 million years ago. The habitat was very lush then. There were large, shallow freshwater lakes, with rich, open grassland on the flood plains and dense woodland beside the rivers. Fossil

61

evidence shows that foodstuffs such as *Leguminosae* (peas and beans) and *Anacardiaceae* (cashew nuts) were readily available, as were *Palmae* (sago, dates and coconuts). Evidence gained from the analysis of tooth markings indicates that our ancestors' diet was much the same as the Guinea Baboon's is today - hard seeds, stems, some roots, plant fibre - a typically tough diet requiring stripping, chopping and chewing actions.

"Our ancestors also had very large molars, with small incisors, unsuited to meat consumption but ideal for consuming large quantities of vegetable matter."

Is the eating of animal flesh bad for health? Yes is the only answer worth giving, for although some people have a better constitution than others, statistics (when produced with an open mind) do not lie. In the same book the statistical evidence of studies carried out by scientists in America: involving 25,000 people, in Japan: involving 122,261 people, in Germany: involving 1904 people, in Britain: involving 4671 people, and in China: involving 6500 people, all confirmed that those who eat animal flesh are more prone to heart disease, and the Japanese studies also confirmed that those on such a diet are more prone to cancer.[3]

For those who are going to cease eating animal flesh, once the body has adjusted to the new diet it usually responds by feeling healthier, lighter, and more vibrant; but if in doubt about what to eat, please consult a doctor or nutritional advisor, and/or join a vegetarian society or group.

In my opinion, the more we aspire toward respect and compassion for all life forms, and for all aspects of nature, the more we advance as spiritual beings. I also believe that at some point in evolution, perhaps as yet several generations off, those who will live upon this planet (perhaps ourselves in future incarnations) will be finer spiritual beings, and this must be so because the vibrational field of the planet herself is changing to become finer (higher), and I don't believe any who will incarnate here will wish to eat the flesh of an animal; as I said in an earlier answer, such behaviour will by then seem just as barbaric and primitive as cannibalism and human sacrifices today seem to us.

18. IS EUTHANASIA MORALLY ACCEPTABLE?

This question is difficult to answer because of the multiple and variable circumstances which will surround each personal case and, because each person, and those emotionally connected to the one who stands upon the threshold, are individual; so a straightforward yes or no, especially from an external source, can rarely be applied; not even when cases might appear near identical.

Firstly, and perhaps the majority who reach the seeming dilemma, the aged, those who might have become infirm, and might regard their worthwhile life to be at an end, feeling that their life has no quality or meaning, and perhaps even finding that the fundamentals of their existence have reached degrading circumstances which they find difficult to accept. If such a person is mentally responsible and able to make their own choice, after due time for deliberation--and a change of mind--wish to terminate their physical existence I, and certainly no spirit communicator I have ever heard or read, would regard this as other than a matter of their own choice, which they are totally at liberty to make. There is no moral jury awaiting in the spirit world, no judge who will condemn or throw scorn upon their free-will choice, for we must all pass from this world, and sometimes it is we, and those who care, who help to extend our intended time upon earth, and this can sometimes be beyond what might have been a natural conclusion.

This reminds me of a poem I wrote as a child, when asked to produce something about the elderly. I cannot remember all of the words, but it started: "Old people are so lonely, they'd like to pass away, but often they cannot, for the doctor's in the way." This, I believe is sometimes why so many reach an infirm condition when, if left to nature, they might have passed without the prolonged torment, which to many it surely is, of an unnecessarily extended earth life. I know that sometimes there might be reasons, and lessons to be learned from an extended life, and this is another reason why the answer cannot be absolute, and the choice must, whenever possible, be left entirely to the individual; for they might intuitively feel whether their time to move on has truly come.

Decisions become much more heartrending for those near ones who see a loved one who is in a position where they cannot consciously make their own choice. Those in coma or unconscious condition, or mentally so far removed to be incapable of such a decision. Here, baring younger cases when a recovery of some kind might still be possible, I feel that a decision based upon what the individual might have requested and wished when in charge of their faculties should be borne in mind. While if their continued physical existence is largely based upon long-term artificial assistance, beyond a reasonable period, then it might be justifiable to bear in mind that, given the opportunity, nature would take them to a natural passing. I know it is easy to say, but based upon what I have learned, those who might be forced to make such decisions should feel no guilt, for 'death' is merely nature in operation; and those whose physical bodies are artificially kept alive are often already living more in the spirit world than anywhere else. Their physical termination will free them to move on to higher levels. While if they are truly meant to return, they will find and be given the strength to maintain their physical existence without artificial assistance. I am not saying that nothing should be done, indeed everything reasonable should be done, for we all need help at times, but there does come a time when the indwelling spirit should be given liberty to move on without restriction, it is their right to choose.

Much of what I have already said can be applied to other cases, such as those who have, or as near as can be certain, terminal conditions. Again, such people should expect no judgment, the choice is their own to make, regardless of the laws of their country, and if the suffering and degradation of their condition is too much for them to bear, they should be given liberty to take an honourable passing. But, before doing so, I would suggest that they search deeply within to see if they feel it truly is their time, or if, even in pain, they still have something to contribute. For, much of the time without realising it, each of us has something to share, even if it be with just one other person, and our life purpose may not be complete unless we stay long enough to fulfil this higher ambition. For each of us is a teacher as well as a pupil.

Finally, when all of the above, and to those concerned much more has been considered, I personally feel that whenever possible, it would be more honourable for the sufferer to take personal control, and not to place an unfair burden upon the shoulders of a loved one, a doctor, or a nurse. Realising that given the opportunity passing is not really that difficult, it only takes a withdrawal from sustenance for a relatively short period, especially when already frail, for a natural passing to occur. Decisions, of course, should not be made lightly, and never in haste, but we have no need of guilt or fear, for all life is eternal.

Chapter Four

RELIGIOUS

Questions 19-24

==

19. WHY DO VARIOUS RELIGIONS INSIST ON THE BLIND DOGMA OF THEIR OWN FAITH, SUPPRESSING THEIR FOLLOWERS FROM SEEKING THEIR OWN TRUTH?

Unfortunately, over the years, and particularly the last two thousand, the lower nature of mankind has gained too strong a grip upon religion. When allowing their true spiritual nature to shine through, people have always intuitively known that life was more than just a physical experience; the natural desire of the spirit within is to seek progression, but for many the physical expression of this desire has become corrupted and more and more materialistic in its craving.

The corrupt of earlier times, including many ancient priests, soon realised the power that was theirs if they could control the thinking of the masses. It was this type of person who took charge of religion, directed it, and were thus able to influence and direct the lives of the vast majority of people. The religious leaders influenced and largely controlled many of the laws, so not only was it very difficult to object to the rulings imposed by religion, it was often against the law, and punishable by death; which today is still the possible outcome in certain countries.

Power corrupts, and the lower nature of man is easily corrupted, and those who seek and are permitted power never relinquish it easily. Those who suppress and insist on others following their faith and laws do so to keep themselves powerful; many follow blindly, knowing no other way of life. With those who object being punished, in one way or another, often, and quite wrongly, in the name of God.

Even in our Western society certain religions have their strict dogma, and it is regarded as very serious if anyone questions certain issues, or wishes to investigate a religion such as Spiritualism, which the orthodox religions fear: because of the truth it teaches, which is so vastly different and the opposite from the controlled approach to God through dogma, ritual and ceremony, which has given the orthodox Christian religion such power, and made both main branches of it (Catholic and Protestant) into such vastly wealthy institutions. The punishment for seekers of truth in our society may no longer be death, but for anyone employed by the orthodox church it could well be dismissal from any position or post held, for even in this country where we consider ourselves free, suppression still exists.

Suppression today is often hidden in falsehoods held and expounded by ministers of orthodox religions, teaching their followers to fear their own personal investigation, and suggesting they may inadvertently become involved in some form of evil. They use this fear as a means of control, although this is often done out of their own ignorance, for they too have been wrongly taught that such falsehoods are genuine causes for concern. It is therefore inevitable to find that those in positions of authority, within the orthodox religions, have never investigated for themselves, and are therefore really not in any position to comment or judge upon the truth of communication

68

and other spiritual facts; those who honestly seek the truth, will always find the truth.

Another form of suppression, which gained more publicity in recent times, is the suppression of women by some religions, denying them the right to hold certain positions of authority, such as priests, within their organisations. Those in charge appear to justify this by referring to the fact there were no women in positions of authority mentioned in the part of the Bible they wish to quote from; a fact which should not surprise them or anyone else, and one which should not be used against women of today. For in biblical times women were generally not allowed into any position of power or authority, such as government, nor allowed a say or a vote. Do these same religions advocate that all such rules should still apply for women of today?

In those bygone days it was good old macho, warmongering man, who ruled supreme; today women have rightly come a long way toward equality; those who live in the past, and quote from past ideology, are burying their heads in the sands of antiquity and not expressing the love they proclaim to live by, under, and in the name of.

Christians proclaim their love and following of Jesus, and yet if we believe all that was written of him, he was never in a position to correct the suppression of women; if he or any person accepted as a spiritual master or teacher returned today they would undoubtedly support equality in all aspects and expressions of life. I could not possibly imagine such a person saying that only men could hold positions of authority, and that women were not permitted such fundamental rights of expression. I believe Jesus was, and in the spirit world perhaps still is, a spiritual teacher, and perhaps a master of such, if only those involved in the orthodox religions would truly open their hearts, and in this way really feel what he would say and do today. Instead, they play around with old words, written by men for men of bygone generations, who did not understand equality, and in most cases did not desire to live with it as part of their everyday, or religious life.

Readers who would like to know more about the origins and development of religion, particularly Christianity, and how those in positions of authority have abused the power they have been permitted, will find my book *Religion: Man's Insult to God* of particular interest.

If we consider what, in earlier answers, I have said about karma, the law of cause and effect, for some, we can begin to see possible undesired karma in the making, for those who are still suppressing women could well be causing themselves future karmic problems. The fact gender is not of any relevance at a spiritual level, and that during many incarnations all people swap sexes, to suit the needs of the particular incarnation, makes for quite an interesting possibility. With the chance that these same men, who are today suppressing women, may themselves become women, who suffer from suppression in a future incarnation. Although the law of karma does not always work in exact duplicates of a situation or circumstance; for if somewhere a lesson has been learned, there is no need to go through the physical experience. Also, the re-balancing effect of karma may not take the same form as the cause, for there are many varied ways in which it can take effect; we must always try to remember that life is for spiritual growth, not for physical detail or revenge.

Before the suppressed women of today begin to rebel too strongly, might I also remind them: that they might well have been the male suppressers of past centuries, now suffering the consequences of their own-built karma. So let us all stop the battle of the sexes, for we do not really know on which side we belong, and on a higher level of consciousness: we are neither male nor female, but a balanced mixture. Even more importantly we should not allow ourselves to be the victims of orthodox religious intolerance, instead each of us should seek personal truth, and throw-off the ball and chain so readily shackled to us by the orthodox religions of the world, along with the hindering restriction to free-thought which they so readily impose.

20. IT IS SAID THAT MAN IS CREATED IN THE IMAGE OF GOD, WHAT DOES THIS MEAN?

What this actually means is that Mankind (not just the male of the species) is created in the image of God, although it is not the flesh and blood of our physical form which is being referred to, it is our spirit. So in essence it is a true statement, but it is one which rather misleads us to imagine God in human form, perhaps with the appearance of an old wise man, and this rather limits our appreciation, while also making us conceited enough to consider ourselves above the rest of creation. God is of course wise, omnipresent, omnipotent and omniscient, but the perfect consciousness we call God is not singularly male nor female, but a perfectly balanced living mind; while indeed *all-life* is created in the image of God, including flowers and trees, birds and bees, all in nature, and all of creation. God is the supreme motivating life-force behind and within all life, and nothing can or does exist without the spirit of God being an aspect.

This wonderful, supreme, eternal force is within and part of us all, and can never be extinguished; so each of us is a miniature version of God; and we each have the potential within to grow and reach the same level as God. To be as God, and at one with God--this is our ultimate aim--and our journey: an eternal one, is a great and wonderful inspirational climb. As we progress and climb our spiritual ladders we can help each other, including those a little behind ourselves, and gradually the whole of mankind will become a finer, wiser and purer reflection of God.

21. IS THERE A HEAVEN AND A HELL?

We are told by spirit communicators that heaven (the spirit world) actually consists of a multitude of different levels (many mansions), all of which are on higher levels of vibration than the earth; the earth herself (or earth plane) is also a level of the spirit world, but one where the vibrations are slow enough for physical matter to form. The higher levels are in other dimensional frequencies, which by many are called the spirit world, these different levels, which can also be referred to as realms or spheres, are levels or divisions between various rates of vibration, the higher the frequency or rate of vibration, the greater the level of progress made by the spirit people who live there.

As we progress, through many incarnations, we gradually move up these levels, as the more spiritually evolved we become the faster our own spirits vibrate, and upon passing, we are naturally drawn to the level which matches our own level of attainment (and subsequent vibration).

These frequencies are easy to describe as high or low, but this is not the ideal description, for they are really just faster and slower rates of vibration. The terminology of higher and lower has given the impression of a heaven above or higher, with the lower levels being less desirable, in time being mistakenly referred to as a place below: called hell.

No such place as hell really exists, not in the sense of a place where spirits are tortured or chained-up in a burning furnace or cave; this idea was merely fostered and embellished by those who wished to instil fear into others, so that they could use the threat of damnation to hell for their own purpose: to demand obedience.

The lower levels, with slower rates of vibration are not so pleasant as the higher levels, and they are the levels to which those who have lived cruel, depraved, mean, nasty and seemingly evil lives upon earth are naturally drawn. But nobody is necessarily trapped within them forever, for all can learn and progress and gradually move-up to higher levels; indeed at our level of understanding: progression through the spheres could be viewed as a reward, for as our spirits gradually become finer we are naturally drawn to move-up to higher levels.

Evil spirits do exist, since we are all spirit beings here and now, and some upon the earth are far from good, and many do seem to enjoy a life that to the majority of us is very much a depiction of a hell upon earth. When such spirits leave their physical bodies for the last time, they are naturally drawn to one of the lower (or slower) vibratory levels; but this is certainly not a hell ruled by an individual, plotting and planning the downfall of mankind. Even if the spirits upon the lower levels had such a collective desire they would undoubtedly be too devious and self-seeking to follow any plan.

Some spirits are so attracted to the earth vibrations and their former way of life, they have managed to ensnare themselves to the earth plane, and they can be attracted to those upon the earth with similar thoughts and desires, for it is a natural law that: *like attracts like*. But this is extremely rare, and is not something that anyone should pay too much attention to, or fear in anyway. For the higher our own thoughts, the higher are our vibrations, and we will quite naturally be protected from any undesired attractions; but if in doubt a simple prayer asking for protection can always be said, and this will bring help from guides and guardian angels.

If we think good thoughts, and live a good life, we will attract good influences around us, and guides and helpers with similar outlooks and personalities to ourselves. They in turn will try to help us in our progression, and when our time to return to the spirit world comes, we will find ourselves being naturally drawn and guided to a wonderful place, far beyond our wildest and greatest dreams.

22 DO EVIL SPIRITS EXIST, AND IF SO, CAN THEY INFLUENCE OR HARM HUMANS?

As will have been seen in the previous answer, I have said: "evil spirits do exist, since we are all spirit beings here and now, and some upon the earth are far from good, and many do seem to enjoy a life that to the majority of us is very much a depiction of a hell upon earth". Therefore, when such spirits pass from earth life they remain evil, and some are so attracted to the earth vibrations, and their former way of life, they have managed to ensnare themselves to the earth plane, and they can be attracted to those upon the earth with similar thoughts and desires, for it is a natural law that: *like attracts like*.

But we should not fear such spirits, for really they are misguided and, for a time, lost souls. They cannot influence or harm anyone who is not of like-mind, and although we are all capable of human weakness, thoughts, words and deeds rarely sink to the level we might call evil. If any reader ever experiences any concern I would suggest they sit quietly and pray to God and their guides for protection, not that there is likely to be any real danger, but it will calm the mind of anyone even slightly worried or concerned; such a prayer should not be considered a weakness, it is as sensible as wearing a seat-belt in a car.

But do evil spirits other than human exist? I can hear readers asking; indeed the mythology of the existence of such creatures has been firmly entrenched into the theology of many religions, and subsequently into the minds of many of their followers.

But with exception to two points worthy of observation, I would firmly teach that no evil spirits, other than misguided human, exist. I will explain my two points of observation a little further in this answer, but first it might help readers to know a little history.

Orthodox religions teach of a leader of evil spirits and demons called *Satan* or the *Devil*, who they teach is in rivalry with God, controlling and directing evil deeds, plaguing mankind; and this idea was instilled into the minds of many ancient and, as they were, easily led people. But the truth is that the idea of a Devil, evil spirits and demons, was only conceived to help those in power (such as ancient priests) to maintain their positions, and to assist their domination of the masses, by offering them protection from evil, and a clear pathway for entry into heaven.

It was a bit like the Mafia asking for payment for protection, when the only people whom we might need protection from, are the Mafia henchmen themselves.

Indeed, as can be read in my book *Religion: Man's Insult to God* the devil is a direct copy of Pan, the pagan mountain goat-god of herdsmen, who was depicted as having horns on his head, and the hindquarters of a goat, complete with hoofs and a tail. The ancient idea of a devil was, in turn, a throwback to nature worship, when the destructive elements of nature were assumed to be the workings of evil gods who lived in the wild, such as in the inaccessible parts of a mountain. When it was a volcanic mountain, the rumblings were considered the voice of such an evil god, who could destroy mankind with a fire like eruption of brimstone. Pan was a Greek god, and Greece not surprising lies in a geologically active region. Once such things are understood and rationalised, it becomes very easy and clear to see why hell, the mythological home of the devil, was always depicted as a place of fire and brimstone, for that is exactly what is found inside an active volcano.

Evil spirits and demons were likewise conjured from the imagination of the ancients, who could not conceive of a single being, even one deemed powerful enough to be in rivalry with God, who could carry-out his 'mission' single-handedly.

So if any reader was concerned about the existence of evil spirits, they should dismiss all worry from their mind, for they cannot be influenced or harmed by mythological figments of the imagination, nor (unless of like mind) by discarnate evil human spirits.

As I said earlier, the foregone answer is with exception to two points of observation; and the first of these relates to people who are living depraved, corrupt or evil lives, and highlights why such people find it very difficult to change.

When someone lives an evil life their thoughts create negative energy, which can form a link with other pools of negative energy, created by those with similar thoughts. Such negative energy can attract the attention of like-minded human spirits, who might try to encourage them to do still more evil deeds. So we almost have a paradox, where a person slips to such a low level of thought they then draw to themselves others who might bombard their thoughts with still more evil; it is a situation which requires much help, so that what good remains, and there will always be some, can eventually be encouraged to develop.

The second point for consideration concerns what might be termed *opening the door*, and the most obvious example of this is when a few friends decide to play with an ouija board. The first question they invariably ask: "is there anyone there" is like opening their front door to whomsoever happens to be wandering by and saying: "would you like to come in for a chat", anyone, good or evil, might do so. In this way even good people can allow an evil human spirit to come close and disturb them, and sometimes the evil spirit might linger within the home, and cause mischief.

It is better for anyone at all worried about such possibilities to avoid playing around with an ouija board; although it is not the board itself which is the cause (for that is merely an inanimate object), it is its use without adequate understanding of what can happen, and without very necessary protection, which can open the door to evil. Rather than telling everyone to avoid using such a tool for communication, because some will always try, I believe it is better that everyone should understand how to use such a tool safely; for when the truth is hidden by those proclaiming to know best it simply causes more misunderstanding and unenlightened dabbling. The truth (or as much as is known) should, in my opinion, always be given; it is the personal responsibility of each of us to decide whether to take heed or, perhaps at our peril, ignore advice.

How to use an ouija board safely is quite simple, it is a matter of ensuring protection; the golden rule is: before attempting any communication or asking any question, always begin with an earnest opening prayer. For the opening prayer is of paramount importance, for it will guard against the intrusion of undesirable spirit visitors. The prayer should ask that with God's love a cloak of protection be placed around all present and over the entire home, and that only good spirit visitors, with the permission of the guides of those present, be allowed to communicate or draw near. Only then is it safe to proceed, with earnest intent to link with relatives, friends and guides to prove continuance of life, not as a game; those who will not take it seriously should be excluded. It is also vital that at the conclusion of a communication, a closing prayer be said, asking to close the link with God's love and protection. If these precautions are earnestly followed on each and every occasion, never forgetting, then nobody should ever be troubled by an unwanted spirit visitor, especially not an evil one.

23. WHAT IS SIN?

My definition of sin is: to behave by thought, word or deed, in a manner which is inharmonious to the indwelling spirit; such behaviour being to a greater or lesser degree, in conflict with the natural laws of God. Murder, robbery, and other such

78

crimes are of course sinful, while they draw us away from the inner love that lies within the core of our spiritual being, and are therefore clearly at odds with the real spiritual us. Which is an aspect of the divine, and must therefore be loving by nature; one day, when we are able to fully remove the outer shell we all encase ourselves within, we will undoubtedly reveal a greater depth of love than we could ever have imagined existed.

Over many centuries, multitudes of people have lived with the label of sin, and the subsequent feeling of guilt this instilled within, often with the seeming pleasures of life labelled sins by those who would wish to be in a position to judge. They have used the idea of sin as a rod, a verbal weapon, to gain control over the masses by creating feelings of guilt, followed by the demand for obedience. With the mental threat of not being forgiven, and the bodily threat of damnation to a hell of eternal torture awaiting anyone who failed to obey the power seeking priests of the orthodox religions of the world.

In my experience: sin is never mentioned by those in communication from the spirit world; advanced teachers simply talk of God's natural laws, and primarily the law of cause and effect, that each will reap according to how they have sown.

As I have said, sin is when our thoughts, words and deeds are in conflict to our own inner being; our higher self knows when we are behaving badly or taking the wrong pathway, or thinking in a manner which does not become us. Therefore sin, and its repercussions are ultimately an offence against ourselves, as God's natural laws are forever in operation, and in time, we cannot help but learn by our own mistakes, and the process of learning can, when necessary, be spread over many incarnations.

Perhaps the original idea of calling something a sin, before the meaning was misconstrued and manipulated by mankind, was really a way of giving a little helpful direction; advice from those who had learned by their own mistakes, and a way of saying that something is perhaps not the best pathway for a desirable and harmonious life of spiritual virtue.

For to live in any way which is not in harmony with our own spiritual yearnings, and higher consciousness direction, can disrupt our finer energy bodies, and for some this can lead to ill health; and this aspect itself could be another reason why the fable of divine punishment for sins developed.

To live in a manner which is contrary to inner harmony is therefore, quite obviously, not a good idea, but it should not be considered that sin will lead to some form of punishment from God. For any repercussions attracted as a consequence of inharmonious thoughts, words and deeds will be drawn entirely by way of natural laws, and not directed from or by a revengeful God; natural laws helping to educate and teach our spirit, and through their operation gradually bringing greater order, balance, and harmony, to our lives.

24. WAS JESUS DIVINE, OR WAS HE SIMPLY THE GREATEST EVER MEDIUM AND HEALER?

Jesus, like all of us, was and is divine. For each of us is an aspect of God, and as such: divine. Jesus is reported to have taught spiritual laws and truths, that life is eternal, and that God is within all life. Since so many of the Bible stories are unreliable, having been subject to interpolations and, over the centuries, numerous rewrites, with no original manuscripts remaining, it is now impossible to categorically state that any of its stories are factual. It is therefore entirely a matter of faith whether anyone believes any part of it. It is also a matter of faith alone as to whether anyone believes Jesus to have been *the greatest ever medium and healer* or a *spiritual teacher or master*. All I can really confirm is that we are all equally divine aspects of God and, although some might have attained to a higher level of wisdom and might, perhaps, be referred to as *spiritual masters*, no master would wish to be worshipped, nor called God.

I do not know how many times from the Bible Jesus could be quoted saying something like 'praise should be given to God', and not to himself, and that 'God is greater'; but instead of adhering to this point it seems to have been twisted round by many indoctrinated people, who seem to regard this as some form of divine modesty. Many of the other reported teachings of Jesus were straightforward advice, based upon the same simple spiritual truths which have always been taught by those with understanding of spiritual laws. They were not the exclusive teachings of one man, but the same spiritual truths which were taught long before the reported history of Jesus, by such as Buddha, and Krishna 1000 years before Jesus, as well as by many others, and are still taught to us today, by those progressed in the spirit world.

Teaching us to *love God*, for if one *truly* puts the love of God into practice, all subsequent thoughts, words and deeds must begin to harmonise with the natural laws. To *love thy neighbour* and *love your enemies*, and the spiritual significance of why this is so important is often missed by people, with even those proclaiming the Christian faith rarely understanding the real implications, otherwise they would surely never have given their blessings to wars and vengeance. For such words of advice not only reflect worthy virtues, they also show understanding of the principle spiritual law, the law of cause and effect. The consequence and teaching of this law is that whatever we say, do or think (cause) will eventually rebound (effect) against us. Therefore the advice (or commandment) to *love thy neighbour* is always the advice given by spiritual teachers, because the consequence of not doing so will ultimately prove detrimental to the transgressor. For if we do the opposite, and send forth negative vibrations, these will circle back to harm ourselves.

It is easier for a camel to go through the eye of a needle, than for a rich man to enter into the kingdom of God and *for what shall it profit a man, if he shall gain the whole world, and lose his own soul?* are really no more than straightforward advice to put spirituality before material profit. For if we spend our entire life in pursuit of wealth, usually to the detriment of others, we will not attain to such a level of the spirit world which might otherwise have been our potential. Likewise *my Father's house has many mansions* is simply illustrating the fact that heaven-- the spirit world--has many levels.

Like Jesus, we are all sons and daughters of God, and have the potential to be as fine an aspect of the God within, as many believe Jesus to have been.

Jesus the man, while upon earth, must have had to learn and work on himself in the same way all people do; I do not believe he was born with, or awoke one day and had, answers to all questions, he would have needed to learn through study, experience, meditation, and communication with those guiding him from the spirit world. Indeed, by the detail reported of his life, if true, it does seem he must have been a natural medium, with excellent clairvoyance and clairaudience. By the stories of his miraculous healing abilities, if not exaggerated, it would also seem he was an excellent channel for Spiritual healing.

But most of all, Jesus should really be remembered as a teacher, who taught spiritual knowledge, truth and wisdom, with the reality of continuous life important to his teaching. I believe it is quite feasible that many of those who were his disciples, likewise were mediums, and if he did return after death in a seemingly physical form, he would have used the energy which they would have been able to produce at their gatherings to do so; and this phenomena is referred to in question 28, concerning physical mediumship.

Spirit world teachers (who regularly communicate through mediums in trance) have many times been asked their opinion of Jesus, and one of the most renowned of these: Silver Birch, in *The Seed of Truth* edited by Tony Ortzen replied:[1]

'There is no mystery about his birth. There is no mystery about his death. He was a man like other men, coming into the world of matter and leaving the world of matter in accordance with the natural laws of the Great Spirit.'

He went on to say:[2]

'He exercised, after choosing the band of men who could help him, those gifts of the spirit with which he was endowed. He was a medium, using exactly the same gifts, spiritual gifts, that mediums are using today. He never tarnished his gifts. His gifts functioned strictly in accord with all psychical law. There were no miracles, no suspension of the natural laws, no abrogation of them and no interference with them. The demonstration of these gifts aroused the attention of the people, and then he proceeded to teach them the simple, eternal, fundamental truths of the spirit which have been stressed by all the inspired teachers throughout all the centuries in which man has trod your planet.

'The rest is known-the incurring of the wrath and displeasure of the conventional and the orthodox. But it is necessary to issue a strict warning that there has been so much tampering with the scanty record. There has been much interpolation, so that all you have is very gravely suspect. You can discount all stories of miraculous happenings, for they did not occur.

'As to the second part of the question, the same individual, the same man-who is not the Great Spirit, not the power which created and fashioned all life and endowed mankind with part of its own divinity-is still at work, still using his gifts and his powers, which have been greatly developed, to help the humanity that he loved and whom he came to serve.

'No service is done to him by abrogating him to a position which he does not occupy, by claiming that he sits on the right hand of the Father, or that the Nazarene and the Great Spirit are identical and interchangeable terms. The Nazarene requires no worship, no servitude, no prostration in front of him, no bending the knee, but only that his life shall be an example to others and that they shall go and do greater things.'

I will conclude this answer by saying: there is nothing wrong with admiring a master, or one perceived as such (and I do personally believe that Jesus, just like Sai Baba who today lives in India, has developed to a point of attainment that is considered a master level), and aspiring to follow their example. To perhaps be slightly crude, many go wrong, metaphorically speaking, by offering worship to the finger which simply points the way when, to repeat, such worship is not sought, desired, or wanted.

Chapter Five

SPIRITUAL

Questions 25-41

==

25. WHY DO SOME PEOPLE FEAR SPIRITUAL COMMUNICATION AND KNOWLEDGE?

Ignorance is undoubtedly the reason for the fear many people hold for what they describe as: "the unknown". They have some vague belief in life after 'death', but are opposed to spirit communication because: they mistakenly believe this disturbs the so-called dead. They sometimes believe the 'dead' have gone to a place of rest, to await a day of judgment, and should not be disturbed until that day comes. They do not understand that the 'dead' cannot be disturbed, because they have never truly died.

When they communicate, directly or more commonly through mediums upon the earth, they are not being disturbed or called-up, they return because they wish to do so. It is usually them who initiate communication, which is not possible without their desire to co-operate; for no medium can guarantee who will 'come through', it is entirely the choice of those from the spirit world.

They return primarily to tell their loved ones that they are still alive, that they can return to visit them; and to show them that they are still interested in their welfare and daily life. If they are ignored, and the chance and opportunity to communicate lost, this can sadden them, if their loved ones deliberately try to forget them, this too can sadden them, for they can see, hear, feel and love, just the same as before their passing.

Many people who are afraid of the unknown would like to keep everything pertaining to the subject quietly 'hidden away' and not spoken of; what they perhaps unknowingly fear (because they cannot consciously analyse it) is the responsibility that spiritual knowledge and truth can bring. For discovery of spiritual truths does indeed bring responsibility, we can no longer blame fate or God for our good or bad fortune. For spiritual knowledge teaches us that every action and consequence of our life is our own personal responsibility; indeed, that it is additionally possible that through the law of karma, we are reaping according to how we have sown in a past life. Understanding the law of karma, cause and effect, gives each of us the opportunity to take command of our life, with a completely different, more positive, and glorious outlook.

It is sometimes said: "ignorance is bliss", and even though it is true to say that if we are truly ignorant we will have correspondingly less responsibility, it is not so if the opportunity to learn was seen, but ignored. For if we deliberately ignore the opportunity to learn, and live in fear of the truth, we will almost certainly have great regret after we pass, for we will then realise what we have missed. After passing there is probably nothing worse than to discover a chance for spiritual progression has been missed; for such progression is our primary reason for incarnation, and it may be a long wait before we have the same opportunity offered in a future incarnation.

Spiritual communications attempt to unveil truth to the world, to give hope, and to support this with knowledge obtained directly from those currently living in the spirit world. To some people this is frightening, for them to even contemplate such truth would throw their whole physical life into disrepute. Their misuse of power, their wrong actions, would be too painful for them to face, for them death is the escape from their actions, or so they think. They also think that by denying truth, and encouraging fear in others, truth will go away, but of course it will not; 'death' is not an escape, it is a time for self reflection, when mistakes and errors, along with good deeds, become crystal clear.

So we should have no fear of spiritual communications, nor of the pursuit for spiritual knowledge, truth and wisdom; for the desire and determination to seek the truth is a most worthy attribute, and one which will, ultimately, bring reward.

26. WHAT IS THE DIFFERENCE BETWEEN PSYCHICS, CLAIRVOYANTS AND MEDIUMS?

Around each of us there is an aura, an energy field, which vibrates and reflects every aspect of our being. It shows our current state of health, emotional and mental turmoil or worries, and spiritual development and growth, plus much more. Through touch the vibration of our energy can be temporarily transmitted to any object, or sensed by any person who comes into contact with it. Items such as clothing, and especially something our energy is in regular or constant contact with, will absorb a stronger or longer lasting vibration. Through contact with another person's energy field, or an object which has absorbed energy vibrations, a psychic can (by using their own vibrational energy senses) attune themselves with these energy vibrations, and by so doing: register feelings. We all have the ability to receive such information (which is encoded within the very vibrations of the energy) but not all of us are able to attune our sensitivity to the correct level.

Psychics are very often born with natural ability to receive impressions, and usually learn (instinctively) to interpret these energy vibrations: but to do so they do not need to link with those in the spirit world; indeed they may not be able to make a communicative link with those in the spirit world.

A medium however: is a person who is able to attune themselves with those in the spirit world. While upon earth we are all spiritual as well as physical beings, it should therefore not come as too much of a surprise to find some amongst us who are able to communicate, spirit to spirit. The difficult part coming in the translation of the communication received: through the subconscious mind, and then relayed to the conscious mind or brain of the medium; for this has to be received in such a way that it can be sufficiently understood, so that it can be passed as an intelligent and meaningful message to the person for whom intended.

One of these methods is called clairvoyance. A clairvoyant: is able to receive communication in the form of pictures, in much the same way we all receive pictures while sleeping. The pictures a clairvoyant receives are usually very clear and strong impressions, the impressions often giving a clue to their meaning or correct interpretation. A developing clairvoyant will gradually build an understanding of what they receive, with one picture or scene very often holding the same interpretation on each occasion received, which enables them to give an accurate message.

Another form of mediumship is called clairaudience. A clairaudient: is able to hear the voice or thoughts of spirit world communicators; the finer channels of this form of mediumship are at times able to pass on messages word for word (although this is difficult to maintain in lengthy dialogue-since once again the subconscious mind is being utilised) which can prove very accurate and detailed.

Another way in which a medium is able to receive communication is referred to as clairsentience, which means: to actually feel impressions upon their body, such as if the communicator had trouble breathing near the end of their physical life, the same feeling can be temporarily given, or transmitted to the medium. Many mediums are able to receive communication combining two or all three of these forms of mediumship, making the message they are receiving (and passing on to the intended recipient) all the more detailed and accurate.

Mediums: are primarily channels for providing evidence of survival after 'death', but will sometimes receive information relating to the future. I would not like to say there are good and bad mediums, all those I know, have met, or seen, try to do their best, but some can attune themselves more finely, and generally put more effort into developing their gift than others.

I have heard some mediums give messages during which they insist that a certain event or occurrence will happen in the future, messages which often make no sense to the recipient, and I can only suggest that if such a message is given to any reader, it would be best if they put it to the back of their mind and not worry about it; for some mediums mistakenly believe that everything they receive has, or will happen; they do not always realise that what they receive may only be a possibility. Everyone has free-will and personal responsibility, and should not sit back and wait for possibilities given to unfold; for lack of action may inadvertently change what otherwise would have been their future.

On what are rare occasions I have also seen some disappointing demonstrations of mediumship, when the medium has even insisted that what they are receiving must be correct, because, they say: "my guide is telling me", and then gone so far as to say: "my guide does not tell lies". Inferring that the recipient is either trying to deny the truth, or are not sensible enough to recognise it; I do not think anyone should have to put up with such behaviour, not during a private sitting (consultation), nor more especially during a public demonstration or meeting. What I would suggest, if this ever happens to any reader, is that they ask the medium if they will pay compensation if the prediction does not come true. The medium may then learn to question what they are receiving, and in time become a finer channel.

Since the primary object of this form of mediumship is to provide evidence of survival after 'death', when a medium fails to express love and compassion, and is only concerned with displaying their own ability, allowing their ego to dominate, they are better ignored until they have learned to put the needs of the one they are delivering the spirit message to, before their own need to be shown in a good light. No prediction for the future is guaranteed to come true: all is subject to personal free-will.

I trust that the last two paragraphs have not put any reader off mediums, for they are as human and as vulnerable as the rest of us; but I did wish to make it clear that standards do vary, and that if any reader should come across a less well developed medium at the outset of their investigations, they should not label them all with the shortcomings of the one, as by far the greater majority are very caring, loving and compassionate people.

27. WHAT IS TRANCE COMMUNICATION AND HOW IS IT ACHIEVED?

Trance communication: is when a spirit world communicator, usually a guide, with permission, uses an earth channel, a medium, for communication; when they generally use the vocal cords of the medium to talk. This is achieved through conscious, or higher consciousness, co-operation on the part of both medium and guide; the medium calms their conscious mind and body to the point where their spirit body is able to leave their physical body: without actually going to sleep, although the condition might initially appear very similar; at this point of co-operation the guide who is to speak blends and superimposes their own thoughts over the subconscious thoughts of the medium.

If the blending is totally successful the thoughts of the guide are able to take precedence over the natural subconscious responses of the medium; therefore the words spoken, and any answers given, are those of the guide, and not the medium. If the blending, and therefore control the guide has over the subconscious mind of the medium is not 100%, the subconscious mind of the medium can interfere, and responses and therefore answers; including, where they exist, prejudiced points of view, can be expressed.

Therefore with trance, as with all forms of communication, we should only accept knowledge which, at the time of receiving, to us has some ring of truth. I would also advise everyone to remain flexible in their learning, for with the passage of time, and further investigation, all knowledge takes on changing degrees of understanding; and what might have been rejected a few years earlier, might later become a cornerstone of acceptance and wisdom. While something which might have at one time been part of our philosophy and understanding of life, might have been swept away and superseded by greater knowledge and understanding.

28. WHICH FORMS OF PHENOMENA MIGHT BE PRODUCED IN THE PRESENCE OF A PHYSICAL MEDIUM?

The manifestations of phenomena which might be produced in the presence of a physical medium can be witnessed by all present, while using normal physical senses, such as those of sight, hearing, smell and touch. Although, because of the complexity and difficulty of blending energies in an harmonious way, which is necessary to produce physical phenomena, demonstrations of this form of mediumship are generally restricted to a small number of dedicated sitters.

The word *dedicated* is also historically very accurate, for some groups have sat together once a week (sometimes twice) for many years before receiving any worthwhile phenomena. While at the outset of sittings to develop such phenomena it has been quite common for groups to sit in total darkness for some weeks or months, until they have received permission to use an infrared light; this is because the energy which is utilised reacts badly to daylight or normal artificial lighting; but once sufficient energy has been established within a room an infrared light is not detrimental to the phenomena (the energies having been manipulated and adjusted to accommodate the light).

When successful the resulting phenomena is undoubtedly worth the wait, for it can take the form of partial or the full materialisation of spirit world people built, more traditionally, from a substance which is mainly drawn from the medium, and called ectoplasm. Although, more recently, some groups are experiencing amazing physical phenomena which is utilising a 'new' (at least to us) purer and safer energy, which is drawn from a mixture of spirit and earth energies.

Other forms of phenomena which can be developed in the presence of a physical medium are such as: *Direct voice*, when all present are able to hear the voice of the communicating spirit. *Levitation*, is another form of physical phenomena, and a person can be levitated, but more generally it is objects which, while remaining under perfect spirit control, can fly safely around the room at great speed. *Transfiguration*, is also physical in definition, and this uses ectoplasm or new energy to build a spirit face over the face of the medium. Last but not least, are the *apport* or *asport* of small objects, which is their materialisation or dematerialisation, when gifts are occasionally given to those in attendance.

These are the main forms of physical phenomena which, over the centuries, have been demonstrated in the presence of a physical medium, producing the clearest and most undeniable proof of continuous life.

The groups which are now receiving and developing *new energy* physical phenomena have found that the guides have not only quickly reproduced the same phenomena, but have gone much further, to produce many new kinds. A great bonus, is the fact that development and resultant phenomena has proven to be much speedier than ectoplasmic development, with phenomena often occurring in months rather than in the years which where often required.

To act as initial pioneers of new energy physical phenomena, a group in Norfolk appear to have been chosen to act as the main experimental group, they are encouraging investigation by established scientists, as well as offering advice to other groups who are successfully sitting to develop new energy phenomena; details of their magazine appear near the end of this book. The founder of the *New Spiritual Science Foundation* Robin P. Foy, in his book *In Pursuit of Physical Mediumship*, highlights the success of this group:[1]

"Members of the Scole Experimental Group experienced 83 different applications of physical phenomena in just 23 months, and this number rose almost every week. The ongoing phenomena included such items as: apports, ringing of bells, mobile spirit lights, levitation, spirit photographic imagery, breezes, temperature variation in the cellar, the sprinkling of water on sitters, spirit writing, sustained spirit lights in glass dome (in different colours), solid spirit entities constantly present during sittings and walking about at will touching sitters, SVOs (self-luminous Sustained Visible Objects), brought about by the spirit team from the spirit world for us to observe, solid spirit entities showing themselves to us in the spiritual light from the dome, spirit lights passing through such solid objects as the central table and sitters bodies, the heavy central table dancing the "cancan" and "energy voices" from spirit speaking to us directly from mid-air or from the solid spirit person themselves.

"So far, the list of phenomena obtained is colossal, but we know that it only represents the tip of the iceberg. Much more is to come in the months and years ahead, as the Scole Experimental Group and the New Spiritual Science Foundation continue with their historic work - a true partnership between our world and the spirit world. I feel extremely privileged to be a part of this unique working group and believe I have finally caught up with the physical mediumship and the physical phenomena which I have been pursuing all these years."

New age technology is also being utilised by the spirit team working with this group, and it is likely that before too long, materialised spirit people might be clearly filmed. One spirit world visitor who has communicated with Robin Foy is none other than the famous second world war politician: Winston Churchill, film of his return to deliver a message to the politicians of today, if he should ever choose to do so, would certainly make world news, and quickly help to spread the truth of eternal life. Meanwhile, he has most certainly promised to dictate a book for publication, using independent voice, and we must look forward to reading this at some time in the future.[2]

29. WHAT DOES A PSYCHIC ARTIST PRODUCE?

Another form of communication: which provides proof of continuous life, comes through mediums generally known as *psychic artists*, although the term *spiritual artists* would be more correct, since what they practice is a spiritual gift. They produce portrait drawings of spirit world people, under the inspiration or guidance of a spirit communicator. The formula of the mediumship used can vary: according to the particular gift and ability of the medium, and the control or method of direction given, or used, by a communicating spirit.

Some artists are overshadowed by the personality of a communicator, and feel they are then drawing themselves, others receive a picture and draw what they are seeing, while others feel their arm and hand is working under the direction of a communicator. Some artists feel they are being used in a slightly different manner on each occasion, and use a mixture of the variations mentioned, so there are no set rules. Although a finely tuned channel, producing this form of evidence, can often produce excellent results: with portraits which can very often nearly match existing earth photographs of returning communicators.

Interestingly, psychic artists sometimes produce portraits of spirit world helpers or guides. While these may not be immediately evidential, until the details are confirmed by other mediums, they are a delight to receive; since we are then able to mentally picture an individual who is giving help and guidance from the spirit world, which is pleasing to the mind, while also helping to strengthen the bond and link.

30. IS REINCARNATION A FACT, AND IF SO DO WE HAVE TO REINCARNATE, & ARE SOME NEW-BORN SOULS?

The majority of us upon earth today are likely to have lived through many incarnations. This is because the life lessons of earth are too varied, and many, to experience in just one incarnation. So in order to learn all of the lessons, that can only be experienced while in a physical body, and are necessary for spiritual growth, we choose to incarnate many times.

Each time we reincarnate it is with a plan: to undertake lessons and experiences aimed to produce greater spiritual growth, with every proceeding life adding to the knowledge of previous lives. This process continuing until all the necessary lessons of benefit to our spirit, which can be experienced while in a physical body, have been undertaken. For some of these learning experiences, we might even incarnate as a member of the opposite to our current sex; this is because gender is of no relevance to those progressed in the spirit world. So we can incarnate many times, swapping gender, in order to experience the lessons most beneficial to spiritual growth and, to suit the needs of the particular incarnation.

The process of reincarnation should not be considered a burden, for in reality it is a blessing, a chance to try again, to improve, and to spiritually grow all the more; with spiritual growth the single most important reason for our life (and lives) on earth. If we only got one chance we would be very limited: as there is not much in life that is easy to learn in one attempt; so to get a second, third and many more chances to progress and improve is very reassuring. Eventually we will all reach a level of knowledge and wisdom which will enable us to be free of the need to return through reincarnation; but even when that time comes, we may choose to return, to help others.

Since we all have free-will, we will not be forced to reincarnate, and there are many who say they do not wish to live another life upon earth. But the real person, the spiritual being we are (which is not encapsulated in the thoughts of our physical brain), will, when we pass and return to the spirit world, use the higher mind, and this will have a much clearer and different outlook.

In the higher state we will eventually comprehend and understand the valuable lessons we have learned through a variety of experiences upon the earth; although memories relating to past lives do not necessarily return immediately upon passing, and I have heard it said that such recall has, in a sense, to be earned; much no doubt depending upon the spiritual attainment of each individual, while for a time expectancy before passing (life's indoctrinated training and thinking) will determine what initially follows. When life becomes uncomfortable upon earth, the thought of returning and doing it all again can be very unattractive, but having returned to the spirit world, a truer understanding of eternity will eventually become more clear, enabling us to put the time span of a physical incarnation into perspective, and we will realise that each incarnation is really a very short experience. So when all is ready, which might be many years of earthly time, undoubtedly many who may at present consider the idea unappealing, will once again choose to continue learning through experiences upon earth, and will reincarnate to do so.

At the same time many are reincarnates, some who are born upon earth have never lived here before, while some have lived in a form akin to human upon other planets, there are those who might be termed: new-born human souls; for creation is never at a standstill, and it never will be, it is forever expanding and developing, with energy changing form and 'new life' becoming manifest. So, although I believe the majority of us currently inhabiting the earth have lived here in human form before, it is certainly not so for all.

New-born human souls have been likened to sparks from God, being released from the creative centre (sometimes called the Godhead), to develop individualised consciousness. Although, it is probable that they and we may have earned the right to this level of existence after evolving through a number of other forms of creation, such as plant, fish and animal, each of which initially have group-soul consciousness. While they might equally have evolved through a form completely different to that of the human, upon another planet, perhaps in a vastly distant and unknown galaxy.

Therefore each and every day, many new-born human souls might come to earth and begin this stage of their personal growth, learning lessons and undertaking experiences for the first time in their current form. While earth is certainly not the only planet of first incarnation or of reincarnation; before coming to earth *each* of us might have lived upon one or more other planets; and likewise, after earth we might choose to be born upon another planet. Whichever route we may choose, gradually, and perhaps through aeons of time, each of us will progress and learn to reflect our true potential, and become a finer aspect of God.

31. IF WE'VE LIVED BEFORE, WHY CAN'T WE REMEMBER DOING SO & WHY DO SOME SPIRIT WORLD COMMUNICATORS SAY WE ONLY LIVE ONE LIFE?

Since we experience life through a physical body, while conscious we generally base all our thoughts and subsequent actions upon the knowledge, experience and understanding developed and stored within the consciousness of our brain. Our brain, being a new physical organ to our current body, and not present during any past incarnation, nor during any time spent in the spirit world or anywhere else, can therefore only remember and reflect upon experiences of our current lifetime.

To remember any experiences from a previous life we would have to raise our consciousness to a much higher level; this can sometimes be achieved through meditation, or some memories might come to us through dreams when sleeping, but these memories are likely to come as fleeting recollections or flash backs, making them very difficult to identify in any certain way.

Many people have accessed information while under hypnotic trance, but here it is difficult to be certain that the subconscious mind is not indulging itself in fantasy, or linking-in or remembering the experiences of someone else.

Although it has been fairly well established that in a large number of cases the information received under hypnosis is from a personal, previous incarnation. The 'proof' often being reflected in fears and phobias of the current life, being caused by actual events of a previous incarnation; such as death by drowning in a previous incarnation, leading to an irrational fear or phobia concerning water in the current life.

Without hypnosis it is generally rare to obtain memories of a past life, as the memories do not usually have any purpose to fulfil in our current life plan; sometimes memories could actually be a burden to our current life plan: as it could be likened to going to school already knowing some of the answers: when it came to exam time some of the lessons would be devalued. Life is therefore planned so we do not have access to certain memories: unless they need to be remembered to release us from adverse effects, such as when fear is carried into our current life, and is causing a phobia.

As for communications which say we only live one life, confusion can arise if the spirit world communicators are considering the question of how many lifetimes we might have led from a different perspective; indeed there are two ways in which they might answer to say we only live once.

The first area of confusion concerns the personality. Where it should be remembered we are eternal spiritual beings, who incarnate into physical bodies to learn through a variety of experiences. When we eventually pass, and return to the spirit world, we understand (eventually, if not immediately) the value of our physical life just concluded, and judge whether it has given us enough experiences to satisfy our need, if not, we can reincarnate and live another physical life. But, if asking a communicating spirit if we the *personality* incarnates again, or has ever lived before, the answer they will of course give is no. For our personality in one lifetime is unique, and we never live more than one life as the same personality.

The other way in which a communicating spirit could give what might seem a confusing or contradictory answer is, when they are considering the question from the perspective of eternal spiritual beings. For when the question is considered in this way, as *eternal spiritual beings* we cannot die, therefore, can only live one life. In other words: our true self, the spiritual being, which in reality we are, only lives one eternal life. For our eternal spirit to view each incarnation as a separate lifetime, would be akin to us considering each new day of our life as separate from, and unrelated to, the preceding days.

So those able to question communicating spirits: must give due consideration to their wording of a question, for if misunderstood, it can result in an answer seemingly contradicting other answers received.

There is also another point to be taken into consideration, and it is that those who communicate from the spirit world are not

101

oracles of *all* wisdom, and there is no spirit world rule which denies those of certain levels the right to communicate. It is therefore quite possible to find that some who communicate are living at a level where the comprehension and understanding of reincarnation has yet to be developed, or perhaps more correctly in many instances, remembered; this may sound surprising, for we upon earth who are seekers tend to imagine that where knowledge, truth and wisdom is freely available none would have doubt, and all would soon learn or remember the truth of such matters. But this is apparently not the situation, for some the inner yearning to seek deeper knowledge lies almost dormant, awaiting a time of awakening, much the same as it does for some upon earth, and nobody forces knowledge upon those who are not ready to seek; while for others, the memories of past lives has been buried so deeply they at present cannot remember all they have previously done. This may sound hard to fathom, but we might relate better to this if we consider that much of what we did as children, indeed sometimes more recently, is lost to our memory. Spirit memory can be held in abeyance, until an individual is ready to embrace such memories as past lives. I have even heard that memories can be deliberately cleared from recollection, especially bad memories, to enable the spirit to grow without the anguish that certain memories might bring.

32. DO WE ALWAYS REINCARNATE IN HUMAN FORM?

To answer this question it might be better to first ask: "what is a human spirit"? The answer would have to be: it is the name given to the spiritual essence of oneself, the aspect of God within which has been released from the creative mind of God (sometimes called the Godhead), which has developed individualised consciousness, this we call a human spirit. The term *human* or *human spirit* is therefore only the name, or label, we give to ourselves to allow us to identify with those we consider, our kind.

I believe many out of the millions of *human spirits* who are currently living upon this planet, have previously lived incarnations upon other planets. This being so, it seems logical to assume our physical form can not only change, but can also change greatly; indeed we need only look at the many differences between the nationalities, and at the differences of colour, shade, size, shape and features between those of one nationality. Although, as far as extra terrestrials are concerned, I believe that in a number of cases there are strong similarities between our general features and their own, which isn't surprising, as I understand those from other planets did help to seed life upon this planet.

It is very unlikely that beings upon other planets describe themselves as *human*, or *human spirits*; whether incarnate, or discarnate and living within a spirit world in the energy field which surrounds their previous planet of incarnation, but in essence they are undoubtedly the same as us, spirits, sparks from God with either group or individualised consciousness. Therefore, the term *human spirit* is restrictive, and in the vastness of creation, and the many lives we can lead, it is most certainly limiting; more accurately, we would be better described simply as: *spiritual beings.*

Can we, upon this planet, incarnate as an animal? is a question which is of interest to many people; yet this is a question which in all my years of experience and investigation I have rarely heard discussed or mentioned by mediums or spirit world communicators. My answer, with restriction and reservation, is yes. My reservations concern two conditions, one: I do not believe, at our present stage of evolution (although this might not have been the case thousands or millions of years ago) it is a common occurrence, and two: I believe it is likely to be restricted to certain more evolved species of animal.

A guide from a development circle I used to attend once told the circle members that he had one such incarnation, as a bear. Having chosen to undertake such an incarnation to gain the experience of living life as a bear, which also enabled him to draw closer to the nature kingdom he still loved. No doubt the experience gave him a unique insight into the feelings, emotions and thinking of such beautiful creatures; he would have learned to understand how they relate to all aspects of nature, to life, to other bears, other animals, and perhaps how they perceive human beings, and, whether they are aware of nature spirits, angels, and other spiritual dimensions of life, along with whether they can conceive of a God. Indeed, all things considered, this sounds like an exciting experience and perhaps one which we might all have needed or wished to experience in eternity. Although, the guide never mentioned his level of attainment when he undertook his bear incarnation, so it might be that it was prior to his human exploits.

The reason why I believe it is restricted to certain species of animal, is because of spiritual evolution, when we progress it becomes more difficult for us to step down the scale of vibration, even to descend to lower levels. Indeed the famous spirit guide whose teachings have inspired many, who went by the name of *Silver Birch*, reported having to use (with permission) the astral body of a native American Indian, to enable him to sufficiently lower his vibration, so that he could draw close enough to reach and communicate through his medium upon earth. This, he said, was because he had progressed to a level of the spirit world from where it was difficult for him to sufficiently lower his vibrations, to directly reach or communicate with the earth plane of existence.[1]

I therefore believe it is either unnecessary for human spirits to reincarnate as certain animal species, because: we have already progressed beyond the need of the experiences and lessons which might be encountered. Or that it is simply not possible, due to the different vibratory rate, for us to reincarnate as certain animal species.

Although which species might be near, at a par, or even above our personal vibratory level of attainment, and therefore suitable for us to reincarnate as if we so wished, is, since we cannot measure or judge, impossible to guess with any level of certainty. But, by what little I have heard, some species which might still be suitable are said to include: dolphins and whales; while in the not too distant past elephants, as well as bears, might have been suitable; and if our concept of beauty has any relation to this hypothesis, then horses could, in the past, have been suitable, along with many more creatures by personal attraction.

Indeed the beautiful and majestic dolphin is mentioned in *The Only Planet of Choice*, which was compiled from channelled information received from advanced spirit beings, by Phyllis V.

Schlemmer and Palden Jenkins. Where it says the dolphin was now the chosen form for many of those who previously incarnated as humans in the region of the earth known by us in legend as Atlantis; it also tells us they (dolphins) are more human than any human on this planet.[2]

While, perhaps more significantly, and still concerning dolphins, it also says:[3]

"They are very sensitive to all consciousness work, but they are also guardians of the seas, and many that oppose the transformation of Planet Earth live in the seas too. They observe and guard, and they also, when necessary, monitor other civilisations of the Universe that approach Planet Earth with questionable intent, and they attempt, because of their great strength of mind, to remove them. They are guardians. They are in service in a similar way that many of you humans are in service, and while their language is difficult for you, it is much better for us."

I conclude the answer to this question, acknowledging, as with many other questions, there is still much for us in mortal human form to learn. Perhaps it is time for all animals, and indeed all creatures which, just like ourselves, are really spiritual life forms, to be given equal respect.

33. IS THERE SUCH A THING AS GOOD KARMA?

What we might term *good karma* is something we are certainly able to create, or earn for ourselves; it is, in essence, the positive outworking of the law of cause and effect. Whenever we show kindness, compassion, friendship or love, we are performing a positive act, and such acts earn the reward of good karma. Our every thought, word and deed will contribute toward our personal karmic account, and when the appropriate moment arises, will rebound to effect us, for better or for worse.

How we think and act will also attract toward us those of like-mind; for there is much truth in the old proverb that birds of a feather flock together. While such attraction will also draw to us those of like-mind from the spirit side of life, and if we think good positive thoughts: we draw the attention of those from the spirit world who feel attuned to such thoughts; while if we think negatively: we can draw the attention of correspondingly minded spirit people; although our true spiritual guides might be, and remain, highly positive in their attitude and efforts to help us. So developing a positive outlook, as well as leading what might be termed a good life, is very worthwhile. For karma is an eternal process, and even if we do not always seem to receive reward during our current incarnation, we will do so in the spirit world or in a future incarnation.

Another point worthy of consideration is that our personal creation of good karma not only helps us individually, but also helps to raise the consciousness of the whole of creation. For in a broader sense the whole of creation is one, having all come from, and being an aspect of, the same divine source: God.

As well as individual karma, there is collective group, national, world, and universal karma, and these can effect what is generally called the *collective unconscious*. With each of our seemingly small contributions, which to us might appear of little importance, playing a part; indeed it is our small collective contributions which go to make up the whole. So we should never underestimate our own contribution toward the collective karma of creation.

As we each help to raise the collective unconscious the effects can indirectly help others; for good thoughts and feelings will flow from us into the collective unconscious, and from there can enter into the subconscious minds of those receptive upon earth and, as this grows, such people will become more likely to respond in like manner. So an upward spiral of thoughts and feelings can be generated, individually and collectively it is up to us as to how much positive energy we give to this and, therefore, to the extent that we are willing to encourage this to develop and expand. Collectively our past and our future destiny and everything this encompasses is, and has always been, in our own hands. Or, more correctly, in our own minds.

By raising the collective unconscious, and through this the general consciousness of mankind, we also make it easier for those from higher spiritual realms to influence us in a positive and constructive way; for the higher our collective consciousness and vibrations upon the earth plane, the closer such evolved beings can draw to us, and assist our spiritual progression, for, in a sense, we will have grown closer to them, and indeed closer to God.

34. HOW CAN THOSE WHO HAVE UNTIL NOW LED A SPIRITUALLY DETRIMENTAL LIFE OF CRIME, SALVAGE OR GAIN ANYTHING WORTHWHILE FROM THEIR REMAINING YEARS?

It is never easy for anyone to openly and honestly admit to past misdeeds and errors of judgment, to search their soul and without any shadow of illusion, confess to what they must consider personal failure. But when such an individual begins to truly accept the reality of eternal life, and realise the inescapable consequences which must follow their every thought, word and deed, to such an offender, every misdeed will indeed feel like personal failure.

But, for such an individual, who has, or is in the process of discovering the true nature of life, and is beginning to realise their life must change if they are to make any true progress (or to mitigate past crimes), there is always hope and a way forward.

For if the dawning of new found belief, understanding, hope, and faith, has entered their consciousness, not through fear of punishment, but through an inner spiritual desire and yearning, a feeling of what is right, worthy and virtuous, then they are already beginning to free themselves from their previously self-built mental prison.

Such desire to change, and to live their remaining years with spiritual virtue, will attract guides and helpers from the spirit world, who will not judge, and although they will recognise and be aware of all past crimes, will only be concerned with how they can help an individual move forward and, spiritually progress during their remaining time on earth.

This of course does not mean all past crimes will be forgiven and the slate wiped clean, for the natural law of cause and effect cannot be fooled, cheated, removed by the utterances of individual or priest, or cancelled by a change of understanding. But if, during their remaining years upon earth, a former criminal, even one still in a state prison, concentrates their thoughts, words and deeds in a manner which is truly worthy of their spirit within, then they might indeed mitigate the karmic consequences of their previous crimes. For, as I said in the previous answer: good karma can be created (or earned) and whenever we show kindness, compassion, friendship or love, do a service for individual or mankind in general, we are creating good karma for ourselves.

Much will obviously depend upon their former way of life, and the severity of their misdeeds, as to whether an individual will be able to re-balance their karmic account during the remainder of their incarnation. If their crimes have been of a minor nature, involving monetary gain without physical harm to others, then this should not be too difficult to re-balance. If, on the other hand, their crime or crimes involved violence, and caused the death of one or more others, then their karmic debt (especially for deliberate murder) most likely could not, in my opinion, be re-balanced during their current lifetime.

Although, if an individual having committed such a crime, is reading this book, and is truly motivated to change, because of an inner spiritual desire or yearning, and not through fear of punishment, then they should immediately begin to put their new beliefs into practise, within every thought, word and deed of their life. For although they might have to correct some of their misdeeds in a future incarnation, through good deeds and service during this lifetime, they can make the task a lot easier.

Remorse, is perhaps the first step upon their new way of life, and even an individual who has little chance to perform a great many physical deeds of service (perhaps because they are still in a state prison), can make some progress. Physically they will be able to see where they might be able to render service; mentally they can develop positive thinking, and perhaps through meditation begin to link more closely with their spirit world guides and helpers; while spiritually, they can pray, and perhaps ask for healing energies to be transferred to those they know to be in need, or to the earth planet in general.

Past crimes do not deny or exclude anyone their right to pray and to link with those in the spirit world, even if they are not consciously aware of a link; we are all nonetheless infinite spiritual beings, and equally divine in our origins. God does not punish anyone, it is the consequences and outworking of natural laws which teach us, and if the lessons are hard, it is us who make them so.

What any individual can say to themselves is: "today is the beginning of the rest of my life", and can consider it the start of a new incarnation; punishment or suffering should only be an aid to self-correction, not as a means for others to take revenge. For who in the course of past and present incarnations (in eternity) is likely to be innocent of all crime? We should at least try to forgive and forget the crimes of those who have, by earth laws, been punished, for we would not wish to be judged by others for our past-life mistakes.

35. WHAT IS THE DIFFERENCE BETWEEN SPIRIT GUIDES AND GUARDIAN ANGELS, & WHAT IS THE ANGELIC KINGDOM?

During the course of our lives, many spirit world people take an interest in us; some are relatives who have gone ahead, who are still concerned or interested in our progress; others include those with a similar personality to our own, who wish to help and perhaps to learn with us. We can also have old friends from this incarnation, and even from past incarnations who draw near. But nearest to us always, are our guide and guardian angel, who are two separate beings, from different lines of evolution. Firstly there is our guide, who has chosen to stay with, or close to us, throughout our current incarnation; along with other guides, who come and go from time to time, as teachers.

Guides try to help us at all times, and all the more during testing periods of time; they can help in many ways, for example: by attempting to influence our mood, by bringing a gentle feeling of contentment, of being light-hearted and joyful, by calming us in moments of stress, and I'm sure many people can relate to a time when they've suddenly been very calm when logically they would have expected to be anything but; while guides might also be able to bring a sense of upliftment when we feel unhappy or depressed. They can also transfer impressions and ideas to our minds, as well as influencing intuition and conscience, and in this way help to guide us, with great care and compassion.

This may sound rather unlikely, and many might think we never receive such help, but for another example: we need only look at the many novelists, comedy and song writers, and many others, who talk of how ideas just pop into their mind. We also receive inspiration while we sleep, in the form of lucid dreams, although on a conscious level we rarely recognise their significance; we can also receive ideas when we are near to or awakening from sleep. Each of us receives help to some degree, throughout our entire life, but often it may seem so natural, because we've always received such help, that we do not realise that we are indeed receiving help. We might think that when we have an idea or a thought we were not consciously trying to cultivate that it is merely the workings of our own subconscious mind, with information filtering through to our conscious mind, perhaps relating to things we have forgotten we heard or read, and on occasions this might even be so, but very often it is our guide who is helping us.

Although on certain occasions and with certain experiences they are not always able to help us; for during our life we have to go through certain experiences, in order to learn from them, and thus develop and grow spiritually. During some of these experiences it might be necessary for our guide to stand back, and simply observe, awaiting the outcome. For they understand that however much they may wish to help, some experiences are necessary for our life learning plan to be fulfilled.

We also have our own free-will, and although our guide might succeed in directing an idea to formulate in our mind, the choice of whether it is ignored or followed is our own personal decision. Whether or not we make a good choice, our guide will continue trying to help us; when necessary, a guide will try to instil supportive courage, and thus help us to face the challenges which are always and inevitably forthcoming in life. If we make a mistake, and choose what turns out to be the wrong pathway, our guide will not become angry or upset, they will simply keep trying to help, with love, compassion, and further guidance.

Similarly, we each have a guardian angel, who is with us from the very moment of our conception, and will remain with us until after our passing; like guides, guardian angels also try to help our spiritual growth; while additionally, they serve as a recorder of our every thought, word and deed, as every response, everyday, in all circumstances, is a form of learning, and our guardian angel will record every reaction.

Our guardian angel works under the direction of those often called *Lords of karma*, and is responsible for putting the karmic law of cause and effect into operation, by drawing to us that which we need to balance our account, and in this way, helping in our long term (eternal) spiritual evolution. This is not to say that the law of cause and effect needs assistance in its operation, it does not, but its effects could take months, years, or indeed a lifetime or more to balance; whereas, with a helping hand from our guardian angel we can clear our karmic account sooner rather than later, and so progress that much more speedily. So in effect our guardian angel is doing us a great service.

Guides are progressed human spirits, who might well have experienced a great many incarnations upon the earth, whereas guardian angels are from a different line of evolution, often called the angelic kingdom of evolution, and they are unlikely to have ever lived a physical incarnation upon the earth. Although angels have assisted, and never ceased, in their efforts to help in the evolution of mankind, since the very beginning of life upon earth.

The angelic kingdom is a wonderful kingdom of creation, who willingly serve and help mankind, and the nature kingdom, and although this is their pathway, they are not our servants, though perhaps they would not object to being called the servants of God. There are many angels, other than guardian angels, who serve in all manner of ways, such as angels who direct healing energies when Spiritual healing is practiced, or whenever healing prayers reach them. Some people refer to advanced human souls as *angels* and even though some may have developed qualities we imagine to be angelic, human spirits do not literally become or evolve to become angels. I also do not believe that angels are likely to appear in human form, for my partner, while in an altered state of consciousness during healing sessions with me, has seen them, and she reported seeing them as pure white-light in appearance, perhaps pure energy beings, and much too bright to be viewed in the same manner in which, during these sessions, she has seen guides.

Under the direction of the angels, and also part of the angelic kingdom, are many lines of creation, there are nature spirits, such as fairies and gnomes; also elemental spirits, who exist within such as minerals, stones and crystals. Once, while I was attending a course which included the equivalent to aura photography on video, I witnessed film, taken in an adjoining room just a couple of minutes earlier, which showed an elemental spirit who moved to the outside of his/her crystal, resembling in appearance a figure like the advertising image used for the film *Ghost Busters*. The elemental figure appeared to suddenly realise he/she was being filmed (or observed), and immediately disappeared straight back into the crystal.

All of creation has life, and is assisted by life, in forms almost beyond our imagination and comprehension in their complexity and numbers. Every single flower, plant and tree is attended by nature spirits, who take to them substance and vital life energy forces, without which they would cease to grow and develop;

the very colour and scent of a flower is only there through the efforts of the nature spirits.

Under the same conditions as earlier mentioned, my partner has also seen nature spirits, and we have even had three-way conversations with some of them. They appear like beautiful little girls about four inches tall, and we have talked with three of them, the first and most communicative is called Lisa, who has long blond hair, and who, while working on the earth, is situated in Ireland, and specialises in Bluebells and Snowdrops. Then there is Claire, who has dark Black or Brown hair; while the third, called Emma, has Black hair, and was seen by my partner to be wearing a green dress and a hat made from a Buttercup, and she reported working with the *green-things* of nature. A Pixie, who Lisa told us works on the earth and potatoes, has also been seen on more than one occasion.

There are elemental nature spirits who exist in the four elements of earth, air, fire and water, each serving and working with purpose, to sustain and develop life. Most of the nature spirits can change size at will, and will do so depending upon the task at hand. We cannot see these wonderful forms of angelic love, unless we have well developed clairvoyant vision, for they are etheric in nature, and vibrate too fast for our physical eyes to see. Although, I believe some angels or archangels have been glimpsed on film taken by those studying lightning storms. For on such films, taken from above the storm clouds, when the lightning has struck, it has revealed images which the storm experts say they are unable to identify. These, I believe, are images (or outlines) of angels and/or archangels, who control and direct storms, while they also direct the nature spirits, who themselves assist in such demonstrations of the power of nature. Although, storms are certainly not

116

manufactured to demonstrate power, they are a way of realigning the subtle energy which surrounds, interconnects and helps to sustain the life upon and of this planet.

I also believe that the phenomena known as *Crop circles* is created by the angels and nature spirits, who use such symbolic shapes and patterns as produced on these occasions to communicate; although, some of these might also be created by caring extra terrestrials. When we do one day learn to read these symbolic messages, I believe we will find they are asking us to stop our destruction of the planet, which they: the angelic kingdom, try so hard to maintain, develop and heal.

If we were to co-operate with the nature spirits, things would be much more pleasant, and life more fruitful and rewarding. For instance: crops should be grown without artificial or chemical fertilisers and pesticides, which the nature spirits dislike. Then by asking, through prayer, for the nature spirits to help in the growth and development of the crops, much bigger and healthier crops would be yielded. The nature spirits desire nothing more than to serve, and to work in harmony with mankind and all of creation, and given the opportunity, and the right circumstances, would do so to much greater effect than circumstances at present permit. Crops grown organically taste better, but perhaps even more importantly, they also have much greater life-force within them, which gives much more nourishment and nutrient to the consumer.

Gardeners, and particularly those who organically grow their own fruit or vegetables, are very often already working in harmony with nature spirits, even if they are not consciously aware of doing so, I would suggest they pray to nature spirits to ask for their help, the results they will then achieve might well give them a pleasant surprise.

Since the angelic kingdom is a subject of particular interest to many readers, in addition to what I have already said, from two books I have selected some passages which might interest readers. First from *The Kingdom of the Gods* by Geoffrey Hodson, which gives many descriptions of angels and nature spirits, as witnessed through the author's personal clairvoyant vision. (To avoid confusion it will help readers to know that Geoffrey Hodson referred to many higher angels as Gods). He says:[1]

"On the lower rungs of the angelic ladder of life are the lesser nature spirits, brownies and gnomes, associated with the element of earth; fairies and sylphs with that of air; undines or nereids with water; and salamanders with fire. Above them, as previously stated, are angels and Archangels in an ascending scale of evolutionary stature, reaching up to the Seven Mighty Spirits before the Throne.

"Countless in their numbers, innumerable in their Orders and degrees, the Gods dwell in the superphysical worlds, each Order performing its particular task, each possessing specific powers and each presenting a characteristic appearance. The whole constitutes a race of evolving beings at present pursuing an evolutionary pathway which is parallel to that of man, and which with him uses this planet and Solar System as a field of activity and unfoldment."

In his book, Geoffrey Hodson, who, by the detailed accounts and descriptions of angels he gives, must have been a highly gifted medium, with excellent clairvoyant ability, mentions a number of angels with a whole range of responsibilities, from caring for a single tree, a mountain, or a large geographical area, to an entire country, while the hierarchy of angelic development: the archangels and planetary angels, care for whole planets, while even higher angels care for the entire solar system; as the following mentions:[2]

"On a single planet such as our Earth, Solar Archangels and angels are represented by corresponding planetary Gods. In addition to these major creative Intelligence's, there are the angels presiding over divisions and areas of the surface of the Earth. They are called Landscape Angels and are partly concerned with creative and evolutionary processes in the mineral and plant kingdoms of nature. A mountain is a living, evolving organism, a body, as indeed is the whole Earth, in which the Three Aspects of the Logos are incarnate. At least three processes are occurring within and about every mountain: the creation and evolution by the action of the Divine Will-Thought of atoms, molecules and crystals of which the mountain is built, the vivification of substance and form by the indwelling Divine Life and the awakening and development of the incarnate mineral consciousness. In each of these, Nature is assisted by hosts of nature spirits and Gods working under the direction of a responsible Official, who is the mountain God. When a peak is part of a range, the whole range in its turn will be presided over by a far more highly evolved Being of the same Order as the Gods of single peaks."

To corroborate the information so far given, I have selected some teachings from a spirit world guide, who is known as *White Eagle*, he was for many years, until her passing, the spirit guide of Grace Cooke, and many of his teachings have been published in book form. I have taken the following from *Spiritual Unfoldment 2*, sub-titled *The Ministry of Angels and the Invisible World of Nature*, where White Eagle is talking of when we, mankind, are finally able to raise our consciousness to perceive other life forms, he says:[3]

119

"you will become aware of the life within the nature kingdom, of streams of life parallel with the human line of evolution, and working with it; of fairies, as you call them, existing not only in children's picture books, but real, and having their own purpose in the scheme of evolution. They are busy carrying the life forces to feed the plants and the trees. If your eyes were opened, you would see some of them in merry, rushing, tumbling, rippling, falling water; these are shining water sprites; you would see sylphs or air spirits on the wing; or in the fire you would see the spirits of the fire, the salamanders."

Evolution does not simply concern itself with human life, nature spirits too can progress, as the following from the same book teaches:₄

"Some of these nature-spirits will eventually evolve to the angelic plane, and follow a parallel line of evolution to the human. As the human will eventually become divine (is essence we are of course already divine, what White Eagle means is that we will become divine in our nature), so certain nature-spirits evolve from gnomes, fairies and sprites to become angelic forms. In the angelic form they play a great part in human life. You are apt to confuse the human spirit with the spirit of the angel. Make no mistake! The angels come through a different line of evolution from that followed by human kind, although it is parallel to the human line, and the angels are closely linked with man and help in his work and life on earth. Man has always walked the earth with angels; the human race, whether it knows it or not, lives through all time under the guardianship of God's angels. It may strengthen and comfort you to know that not one of you treads the path of life alone; for from the moment of birth until physical death, you are guarded by an angel appointed for that task."

The final passage I have selected from the same White Eagle book, touches upon the same vast complexity and grandeur of the evolutionary plan as the final passage quoted from the Geoffrey Hodson book; and might somewhat justify his term of *Gods* for highly evolved angels. It says:

"Angel beings came to earth from Venus to assist in the beginning of this earth planet, and in the creation of the form-life on this earth. As time passed there came also to the earth those *human* beings who, having reached a certain stage on the path of evolution on another planet, were more advanced than souls then incarnating on earth. These more evolved souls assisted the younger ones on earth. Thus there came the two types of beings concerned with the creation of the earth life. There were the angels or the great planetary beings, who may be referred to as Gods; and those advanced in human evolution-God-men.

"We have many times referred to the Three, who have always been since the beginning; Who are concerned purely with this solar system and the evolution of the earth planet, and Who are best understood as the three aspects, Wisdom, Love and Power. These are the Three from Whom all life comes-the three first or major Rays of life. On one of these three Rays comes the angelic line of service, concerned with life form throughout *every* kingdom."

Both books I have quoted from go into far more detail than I could possibly accommodate into this answer, but suffice it to say, we are not alone in our evolution, which is far grander than we might ever imagine.

36. IS THERE A DIFFERENCE BETWEEN THE TERMS: SPIRIT, SOUL AND GHOST?

Firstly, I will look at the terms *Spirit* and *Soul,* which most people so closely associate they are often considered to have the same meaning; although, strictly speaking, their meanings are not identical.

Our spirit is, in essence, a divine spark or aspect of God, which has been released to develop and evolve to individualised consciousness, and then onward upon the spiritual pathway; or, we could say, our spirit is the pure indestructible aspect of God which we might consider our super-consciousness mind. Whereas, our soul: is the ultimate expression of form our spirit manifests through, and can also be called our celestial, heavenly or spirit body, and is associated with, or the highest aspect of, the permanent body we use in the spirit world. Our soul, or an aspect of it, can therefore take many forms, changing in appearance from one incarnation to the next, to look identical to our latest physical form. So soul is substance, but it is eternal, indestructible or divine substance. So the spirit and soul go hand-in-hand, we cannot have spirit without soul, nor can we have soul without spirit.

When we pass, and return to the spirit world, we generally continue, by a quite natural process, to use the appearance of our latest incarnation, although occasionally, or in time, we might choose to use the form which was ours during a previous incarnation. Though our soul, or soul body, is of much greater significance to us than our physical body could ever be; for whereas upon 'death' our physical body will disintegrate into seemingly insignificant, although recycled, particles, as I've said, our soul is eternal, indestructible, and flexible; indeed we, like the fictional characters in *Star Trek: Deep Space Nine*, are *shape shifters*.

I once asked a communicating spirit whether, on the really higher levels of the spirit world, the spirits there continue to use a soul body of similar appearance to the physical form, and was informed that some do not; instead they appear like a wisp of fine mist, for such is their progression they no longer have the need to use a form recognisable to us, although they could, if they so wished.

Moving on to the difference between a *spirit* and a *ghost*, indeed by most definitions if someone was to say they had seen a spirit, or a ghost, it would be assumed they had seen the same thing: either someone returning from the spirit world, or the sighting of one classified as an earthbound spirit, which is someone who, for one reason or another, had not left the earth plane level of existence.

But these two terms might be better employed in two separately definable ways, to give a clearer and more immediate understanding of what has been seen, with the term *spirit* used to refer to the sighting of a conscious living soul, while the term *ghost* could be used to refer to the replay of events which once occurred.

For upon the ether, which is the name given to the energy which fills all space, all events are imprinted. Sometimes these events, especially those which involved strong emotions, or alternatively those which occurred during certain atmospheric conditions, such as stormy nights when static electrical energy gathers in the atmosphere, seem to be particularly ideal conditions for imprinting events, in such a way, that upon our earthly level they can, on occasions, be seen and heard to replay.

Little is presently known as to why such events might replay on certain occasions, such as a time when conditions, like the stormy nights previously mentioned, occur. Although what does seem likely: is that these conditions tune the ether to the waveband (frequency) of the past event, causing or supplying the ideal conditions for it to replay.

But additional to this type of atmospheric replay, some events seem to be linked or tied to a time cycle replay, when events replay on what seems a pre-set timetable, such as the same night annually, like a recording set to replay at that specific time.

Very little is presently known about ether cycles, and indeed all life is governed in cycles, as Numerology teaches, but at present detail of how these cycles work or operate on spiritual or cosmic levels is not forthcoming. Frustratingly, even those of us who receive communication are not taught everything: perhaps because our guides don't have all the answers, perhaps because while we are upon earth such information is superfluous to our needs and ability to comprehend.

A figure who is seen to float down a corridor, with legs and feet appearing to run through and below the floor, or alternatively who is in mid-air, sometimes with their head going through the ceiling, could be defined as a ghost. For such a figure is merely an action replay of some event from the past, the actual person, the conscious living soul who was originally involved, is no longer present, so of course no conversation could be held with such an apparition.

The reason why a ghost might appear to be floating above a floor, or be seen with legs passing through and below, is because when the events actually took place, and were imprinted upon the ether, the original or previous building had floors at a different level to the present day construction. The replay is frozen in the same space in the ether, it cannot adjust to the new or altered building. This is also why ghosts often appear to walk straight through a wall: when the event actually occurred and the imprint was made, there would have been a gap or a doorway in the spot they are seen to pass through. This, of course, is not to say a conscious living spirit, returning to visit earth, could not also pass through a wall, for since they are on a different level of vibration, they can.

37. IS SPIRITUAL HEALING BENEFICIAL?

Spiritual healing can potentially help any problem, whether it be in mind, body or spirit. It is a method of channelling healing energies, under the guidance and direction of spirit world guides and healers, through (in broad terms) the spirit of the earth healer (who is simply a channel), to the spirit of the patient. It is a simple, natural and safe process, which can, and should be used world-wide for the benefit of mankind. For since all people are truly spiritual beings, the practice of spiritual healing is an ideal way to give help when and wherever needed.

With Spiritual healing, what actually happens when a healer prays to be used as a channel, and places his or her hands close to or upon another, is that spirit guides and healers hear the prayer, and are able, with the help of angels of healing, to direct a flow of healing energies (which to a clairvoyant appear as coloured light rays) through the spirit (or soul) and finer energy bodies of the healer, to the spirit, mind and body of the patient.

Since mind, body and spirit all inter-connect, when one aspect of being is out of harmony it can also adversely affect another, therefore if we are upset, or stressed, emotionally or mentally, this can manifest in our physical body, in the form of ill-health. Spiritual healing can help to re-balance and harmonise through our spirit and finer energy bodies, producing harmony within each, which in turn can enable our physical body to begin its recovery.

To produce this effect the incoming healing energies flow through the finer energy bodies of the healer, and out, usually through minor chakras in their hands (although other chakras can at times be engaged) to the patient; where the healing energies flow through their finer energy bodies, and can enter their physical body via their etheric chakras, from where the healing energies can pass to their glands and along meridian pathways to their organs and other areas.

The beneficial results of Spiritual healing have been documented by a number of healing channels, including the most famous of the twentieth century: Harry Edwards, who reported some of his healing successes in a number of his books, including *Spirit Healing* and *The Power of Spiritual Healing*. Indeed, there are many cases on record of miraculous cures being obtained through the application of Spiritual healing. For example, in the second book mentioned above, a case is on record where a patient who was diagnosed by orthodox medical practitioners as being beyond help with an inoperable cancer tumour who, after they received Spiritual healing, was able to make a complete recovery, with the cancer tumour shrinking and completely vanishing.[1]

Spiritual healing can also be practiced at any distance world-wide, and non-contact healing is, by many, known as: *Absent (or distant) healing*. The process of transference of energies is not limited by physical separation, for the whole of creation (being an aspect of God) is in one sense linked, or one, this

126

connection allowing energy to be directed anywhere, at any time, without hindrance.

I myself practice Spiritual healing, and any reader can, if they so wish, write to me for Absent healing, for themselves, for others, or for pets. It is not necessary for me to know the symptoms or problem, but they can be given if the writer wishes to do so; the address of where to write is given near the end of this book.

There are occasions when Spiritual healing may appear to fail, for healing energies will not prevent a passing which is destined to take place. Additionally, if someone has been born with a life plan which involves going through a certain experience, this too may prevent response; for if Spiritual healing were allowed to take away the problem, the lesson the person was to learn would be diminished or denied to them; something which they would regret upon their eventual return to the spirit world. It is therefore not in the spiritual plan of everyone to receive the full benefit which is possible through the application of Spiritual healing. Although, if a life lesson which causes or includes a particular illness or problem has been learned, then the healing energies might very well be able to produce a change or improvement.

We should never conclude that someone who fails to respond to Spiritual healing is undeserving, for lessons: which we are all here to learn, are often very subtle and hard to fathom. It is indeed very difficult for us on the physical level to fully appreciate the reasons for certain lessons; so we should never judge another, or try to justify their problem. If someone fails to respond to Spiritual healing we should only feel regret and sympathy and, encourage them to be positive and never give up. For as many factors which we cannot see with our limited view and understanding change, develop or progress, the healing energies might, on a future occasion, prove effective.

Of course not all illnesses and problems are in the nature of spiritual lessons, there are a multitude of possible reasons for ill-health, and the same problems can arise if we fail to look after our physical bodies. While there can also be an element of good or bad fortune involved, with rogue and unhealthy cells in the atmosphere. Spiritual healing can potentially help in all circumstances, but if the problem is caused by certain behaviour or action, or even a certain thought process, which continues after Spiritual healing has begun, the treatment may not be effective or its results long lasting. For a straightforward example: if someone receives Spiritual healing for a strained back and, afterwards, because they feel better and stronger, they immediately start lifting heavy boxes, their action will very likely undo the benefits received. So we must all consider our own personal responsibility, Spiritual healing can and does help, but it is rare to get a miraculous or instant recovery, most responses are in relation to the problem and, a long term or more serious problem will usually take longer (and more sessions) to respond than a more recent or minor problem. Although, on occasions, miraculous cures and seeming miracles can and do happen.

38. WHAT IS PSYCHIC SURGERY?

Psychic, as it is more commonly called or, as it should really be termed, Spiritual surgery, can be compared to Spiritual healing, in the sense that it is a method of healing under the control of spirit world healing guides. But with this form of healing, what often happens is that the healing medium, the earth channel or instrument as they can be called or referred to, might be controlled in a trance condition while, through them, the guides or spirit doctors might perform operations which can be similar to orthodox earth surgery.

The controlling spirit healing guide who, behind the scenes, is assisted by other spirit healers, with spirit vision (not the channel's eyes) is able to see the physical or energy problem within the patient, so there is no guess work concerning their condition, it is clearly visible and understood. This, like Spiritual healing, does not always mean they are able to rectify or heal problems in one attempt, if at all, for once more many possible factors can influence what might be achieved.

The spirit healers are able to influence and control energy, or they can operate directly upon the physical body; to do so they sometimes use surgical or improvised implements; sometimes these are unseen spirit created surgical implements, which can be inserted through the flesh of the patient to carry-out an operation or make some internal change, and this is often done without making any visible incision. While some spirit healers will make an incision which, after the surgery, is closed and healed, leaving no (or only a very faint line which later vanishes) sign that the body has ever been operated upon. Indeed, surgical implements, blood and other parts (even organs), which have been removed or replaced within the physical body can dematerialise.

A reported account, which I shortly quote, mentions a new---made in spirit---heart being materialised and transplanted within a patient, while the original simply dematerialised, and this concerned the Psychic surgery of Stephen Turoff, who currently practices in Chelmsford; and whose hands are used predominantly by a Doctor Joseph Kahn, from the spirit world. I say *hands* because Stephen Turoff is often conscious rather than fully entranced during his surgery, while the doctor controls his hands, Stephen Turoff, jokingly, describes his role as at times being "like a puppet".[1] The following is taken from the Summer 1996 issue of the *Kindred Spirit* magazine interview with Stephen Turoff, concerning a lady from the Canary Islands:[2]

"She came to see me with a bad heart complaint. Her doctor had taken X-rays and warned that the heart could give out at any time. Dr. Kahn worked on her for three consecutive days-a few minutes each time. Then he told her to go. I heard, through a friend, who flew over a few weeks later to see me, that on arriving home the lady had been feeling much better. She had visited her doctor for further tests - without having mentioned the trip.

"After various X-rays and scans, the doctor became agitated and called in a professor. After they had both looked at the new results and compared them with the old the doctor said: 'Who are you?' She replied, 'I am Mrs....Doctor, you know me.' 'But you can't be', he said. 'I am', responded the lady, 'Why are you asking me this?' The doctor, ashen white, replied: 'We can't understand it. Your heart is fine, but it's not the same one.'"

Dematerialization may sound like science fiction (more *Star Trek*) but when the vibratory rate of any matter is increased sufficiently, it will quite naturally disappear from the visual spectrum of our eyesight. What is more remarkable and exciting is, the new (new energy and spirit technology appear to be involved) ability displayed by the spirit doctor's: to create new organs---and to materialise them in the physical dimension---this is, I believe, unique in the history of Spiritual healing or Psychic surgery, and is most likely a breakthrough in spirit world healing ability.

It is also possible for some Psychic surgery to take place during Spiritual healing, without the necessity of the healing channel being controlled in a trance or semi-trance condition. For this to happen an energy field is created, often between or near to the channels hands, which allows the spirit healers to perform surgery within this field of energy.

So there are no definite rules of operation, all is dependent upon and subject to the capacities of the healing channel and, preferred method of procedure chosen by the spirit guides; which itself might well be subject to the conditions they (the guides) can generate and feel happy or, have to be contented with.

39. IN THE SPIRIT WORLD, DO THE PEOPLE THERE HAVE BODIES LIKE OURS, & WHAT IS THEIR WORLD LIKE?

By my understanding, the people in the spirit world do continue to use a body; they use an aspect of the soul body, and this is as real and tangible to them, as our physical bodies are to us.

The exception, in appearance, might be those who have evolved to an extremely high level, for they have no need of the outward physical appearance we have grown accustomed to. They still have a soul, but to those from the spirit world who have communicated the information, they describe it as 'mist' like in appearance.

But those spirit people who have not yet reached such levels of attainment, their bodies are duplicates of the physical bodies they used upon earth, but with any defects eliminated. For example: if someone had a physical body which was scarred, missing a limb, or unable to see when they passed to the spirit world, all of these defects would vanish. Even if they were born with a deformity or handicap, scars vanish, missing limbs are no longer missing, and those who were blind are able to see. In other words we return to being as perfect as we were, or should have been.

The soul body, being a spiritual body, cannot have any of the problems which might have been experienced upon earth; it is a perfect body, and as such does not become ill nor can it be harmed, not in any way. Furthermore, since it is motivated by spirit, it cannot age, as there is no age as we might appreciate it, in the spirit world.

Because it is ageless, those who pass in old age revert to an appearance from their prime, while those who pass young mature only to an appearance they are happy with, and not beyond. The perfect system we might say, and why not, it is heaven after all.

As for what the spirit world is like, well the descriptions do vary in detail, but we should expect this, as not all live on the same level or in the same location. The problem would be similar to two people describing to a third party a country the third party had never visited, and had no knowledge of; and to compound the problem, the two people having stayed at different ends of the country, the differences might be vast and varied.

Although, what each spirit world communicator does confirm, is that everything is harmonious, peaceful and beautiful beyond our imagination. There is countryside in abundance, magnificent trees and greenery, beautiful flowers, friendly animals, and birds singing, a paradise for all to enjoy. There are lovely country cottages and houses for those who desire and deserve them; even clean and tidy towns: for those who feel happier in such an environment, something for everyone.

If we were to look for a location for the spirit world, it has often been described by imagining several rings around the earth; with each ring representing a different level; with the rings which are nearer to earth being the lower levels, and the ones which are further away the progressively higher levels.

The power of thought is used for the building of all things, including property. But such tasks are undertaken by experts, one or more who have trained their minds and, can direct their thoughts in such a controlled manner, to produce the desired effect; without, of course, the physical need to lift a single brick or stone. Some of the homes apparently have no roof, since there is no need for one, for bad weather and rain do not exist there. It is never cold, nor too hot, it is like a continuous and perfect summer day. Readers might come across some spiritual books where the spirit world is always described as the *Summerland*. It is also a world of light, with no night, no darkness, only shades. Sleep is not necessary, although people can relax and rest in a sleep like state if they so wish. Food and drink are also not necessary, as the soul body does not require it, although once again some can be taken, if the desire still exists. Travel is also reported to be a simple process, with this being achieved by mental projection, all one has to do is to think where they wish to be, for them to be almost instantly there.

I look forward to being able to go for long country walks, perhaps with a pet cat for company. Pets too, do not need to worry about food, so earthly problems and planning will not be of any concern. There is also no danger to pets from other animals, as all are tame, and of course could not cause harm even if they wished. On most levels there are no cars (although on the lower astral some might still be created through desire), since there is no need for them, so they do not present a problem, and it is impossible for a pet or a person to become lost, as a mere thought brings one to where they wish to be.

There are also a multitude of pastimes available for all to engage themselves in, so there is never any need to feel bored. For instance: one can learn to cultivate flowers and plants, or to express themselves through any form of art or music. If someone simply wants to read or study, I have heard it said there is a copy of every book, ever written, throughout history.

If someone wishes to return to help those still upon earth, they can also be trained in this. They do not even have to worry if the one they wish to help speaks another language, for in the spirit world the memory is infallible (the mind, rather than brain, being used), which makes learning much quicker and easier. Although many communications between those in the spirit world and earth are through telepathic thought transference, which can automatically translate itself, via the subconscious mind, into an understandable language for the receiver.

So as will be gathered, life for those in the spirit world is in many ways infinitely more satisfying, and rewarding, than life upon earth. But before anyone starts to wish they could make a quick return to the spirit world, they should consider the fact it was them who chose their present incarnation (with possible exception to new-born human souls). Also, whatever experiences we may go through upon earth, will benefit us greatly when we eventually do return to the spirit world. We should try and savour and enjoy every minute, for even in the seemingly bad experiences, there is always something for us to learn. Everything is of importance, and in time, even the worst experiences may turn out to be our most cherished memories, for they might be the very times which have taught us the most, and through which, we have made our greatest spiritual progress. Our current incarnation is a unique experience, something which will eventually seem like a fleeting moment in time, so we should make it a treasured moment, by using it wisely.

40. IS PRAYER BENEFICIAL AND IF SO HOW SHOULD WE PRAY?

The power of prayer is a great and wonderful thing, and should be used on a regular basis. It works best when our prayers are a sincere thought and gesture, coming from our heart. They should be said for enlightenment, support, guidance, encouragement, protection and many more needs, but always for a high ideal and motive. But perhaps the most important use of prayer is for healing.

For our prayers to reach God, or spirit world guides and healers, or loved ones who have gone ahead, they should be a gentle, but concentrated mental projection of our thoughts. There are no strict rules to composition, the wording should be based upon personal experience, if it feels or sounds right, it is right. I personally find it easier to mentally project the words rather than saying them orally, and the object is to transfer thoughts and desires to those in the spirit world, and they communicate on a telepathic link, although I'm sure that either method can be equally effective.

Those who have never grown accustomed to the art of praying, and would like to try, perhaps to pray for healing for those they personally know who are sick, as a simple guideline: I would suggest they go into a quiet room, relax and close their eyes, then begin, for example: by asking that healing should be directed or given to those known to be in need, naming them in their mind, or in the same way asking for healing to be given to the earth spirit herself. There is no limit, and distance is no object; out of courtesy and good manners, I believe we should never forget to finish by saying thank you to those listening.

All prayers should be of good motive and with an open nature, and never seeking an unworthy outcome. Healing prayers can ask for healing for anyone, anywhere, but our prayers should not ask for a specific outcome, merely for all that can be done, to be done, allowing those who help to judge the need and amount of help that can and should be given, for they are in a much better position to evaluate the need with spiritual vision and perspective. What would be unworthy, would be a prayer asking for personal acquisition or financial gain, just because we might enjoy it; but a prayer for financial help for self or others when in real genuine need, rather than a want, would be worthy.

This does not mean all seemingly justified prayers will be answered in the way desired, they will be heard, and not ignored, but there might be reasons why help cannot be given, such as a karmic situation. There are also many plans which cannot be seen with physical perception; plans which interweave many thousands of people together, even for a short period of time, and what effects one might have a knock-on effect upon others, so from the physical level it is often near impossible to fully understand why many things happen or do not happen.

To conclude, I would urge all those who have the desire to pray, especially healing prayers, to do so; for even the seemingly unanswered prayer will be of benefit in the long term. Even if results are not immediately obvious, before too-long, those who begin to make use of prayer might begin to intuitively feel, and will certainly see or hear whether their prayers are actually bringing benefit to others, indeed success to some degree should be anticipated, for prayers are a great and wonderful power bestowed upon all mankind, and everyone of us can, if we would but try, bring this universal power into beneficial effect.

41. CAN SPIRITUAL GIFTS BE DEVELOPED?

Some people are born with what are termed natural gifts, they are able to see, hear or sense spirit world people; or, in some way, they can intuitively use their psychic abilities. Indeed gifts can, of course, take many forms, and herein I mainly concentrate upon mediumistic gifts.

I believe the majority of those with such gifts were born with their gifts developed to some degree, so that they could use their gifts for the benefit of others; having earned the right to be born with their gifts developed to a greater degree than the average person, because of their spiritual attainment, earned and established by their efforts and progression during previous incarnations.

But a far greater number of people who eventually develop gifts begin with no obvious gift, and many such people enter their maturing years before their development begins or unfolds. While others go through their entire life without developing the latent potential within, often because they are unaware of the fact that gifts can indeed be developed.

We are all spiritual in nature, and as such have some potential, with each of us linked to higher levels of consciousness than generally realised. For we each have seven main physical linking chakras or energy centres, which are sometimes called psychic centres, and these centres link with finer energy bodies, or fields of energy, which surround and inter-connect with our physical body, and with our higher level of consciousness, often called our *higher-self*. So there is nothing to prevent each of us from developing to some degree, and at times we do all use these centres, for instance: from time to time we all receive intuitive ideas; and these can be thoughts relayed to us, via our subconscious mind, from where they pass to our conscious mind, without us having to make any conscious effort to formulate an idea.

Some of us will quite naturally develop gifts quicker than others, and some will develop one gift to a finer degree than another. For we are all different, and at varying levels of personal spiritual development or attainment. If we wish to develop gifts, motive is of paramount importance, for instance: if we wish to develop the gift of Spiritual healing, we will be more likely to succeed if we have the right motive. Which is the desire, with compassion and love, to serve and help those who are suffering, without any need to boost our own ego; with the help we can give being far more important than our reputation. The same principle can be applied to all potential gifts, we will have a much greater chance of success, if we wish to develop only for the good we can do, and not for the aggrandisement of self.

Another point which needs consideration, is the fact we cannot necessarily choose which gift might be developed. Through prayer we can offer ourselves in service, and if we undertake this with sincerity and honesty, and with the right motive, our prayer will not be ignored. But, those who guide and work from the spirit world, will be able to see wherein our greatest potential lies, and will attempt to bring this into service. So any latent potential we might have to develop and use a gift, might well, in fruition, turn out far different from what we might have originally envisaged.

One of the best ways for us to begin the process of unfolding potential gifts, is to sit in daily meditation. Where possible it would also be a good idea if we were to join a development circle, most of which sit as a group once a week. Ideally these are run by a developed medium, but if one is not available, there is no reason why some like-minded friends should not get together, to form their own small group. Ideally no more than seven should be in the group, with one taking charge. Harmony, or as near to it as possible, is important, and anyone not blending in should be politely asked to leave. I would also recommend that any new group, without a developed medium, start by asking to be used for healing, to help anyone they know who is in need, or the earth spirit herself, and the meditation should always be opened and closed with a prayer, asking for God's love and protection.

Patience will be required, for many of the mediums who today practice their gifts sat in such circles for many years, before being confidently able to demonstrate in public. Wise mediums also continue to sit in circle, for no matter how proficient they may have become, the unfolding of spiritual gifts is always an ongoing process, and sometimes other gifts may develop at a later time.

Even though each of us has some potential, it is not the intended plan that we should all develop mediumistic gifts such as clairvoyance, clairaudience and healing, during our current incarnation. For some of us are born with other lessons and experiences to undertake, and of course there are other gifts which are equally spiritual in their own right, and which are important to mankind, such as art, music, poetry and comedy, which themselves can be therapeutic, and a form of healing; with laughter certainly being a great tonic for any ailing spirit.

Meditation is beneficial, even when it is not used to aid the development of spiritual gifts; for it can relax the mind, and put us at ease, reducing stress; thereby meditation is potentially beneficial for our health, and leaves us in a better position to make constructive judgements. It also sows good seeds for our long term future, as no experience is ever wasted, and additional benefits might be reaped during a future incarnation, when the development of gifts might, with greater ease, be achievable.

Chapter Six

ODDS & CURIOS

Questions 42-47

===

42. CAN COLOURS, CRYSTALS & MUSIC HAVE BENEFICIAL EFFECTS UPON US?

Colours, Crystals and Music can indeed have beneficial effects upon us, and particularly with colour our language reflects this, with it used to describe a variety of feelings and emotions, such as *off-colour, in the pink, feeling blue, seeing red* and *green with envy,* while someone deemed a coward is often called a yellow belly. Each chakra or energy centre of our finer energy bodies vibrates at a range of frequencies similar to that of a colour, with the range of the seven main physical linking chakras: from the base to the crown, having their own representative colours. These are as follows, base: red, spleen: orange, solar: yellow, heart: green, throat: blue, brow: indigo, and crown: violet. With each one of these in turn corresponding closely with one of the seven notes of the musical scale. All contact with colours, even seeing them with our eyes, affects us to some degree; additionally we can absorb vibrations from the colour of clothing worn, the decoration in the home or work place, or from the colour of the food we eat.

Basically the colours which correspond with the three lower chakras are warm colours, namely: red, orange and yellow, which activate and stimulate, giving energy and strength. While the colours which correspond with the three higher chakras, are cool colours, namely: blue, indigo and violet, which calm and sedate. With green, which is at the heart centre, being neither warm nor cool, but a balance point between the two halves.

Colour can be used in a variety of ways, such as: to bring a feeling of upliftment, and by brightening our mental outlook: through our choice of colour worn; or used in house decoration to create a relaxing atmosphere. Incidentally, the room where I wrote much of the original *Golden Enlightenment* manuscript had a gold glow to it, which is good for higher aspiration thoughts, while it also gave me the idea for the first word of the title. Colour can also be effective and more directly beneficial to our health, for example: we can select an appropriate colour to place in our energy field, and over a particular chakra, to either calm or stimulate our vibrations. While breathing with colour, that is, to imagine each of the colours in turn flowing into the body while taking, and holding for a few seconds, deep breathes, can be energising and therapeutic. A cleansing colour or white light can also be visualised flowing to any area of particular concern.

Crystals and gemstones are currently becoming more recognised (or rediscovered) for their healing quality and, the general upliftment they can bring. There are a variety of crystals which can be related to each of our chakras, and if placed over, or in close proximity to them, can help to re-balance them, and thus aid self-healing. Crystals, gemstones and, all rocks and minerals, carry their own vibration, which, like colour, if used to their potential, can be of great benefit to mankind. For example: clear Quartz crystals can protect and promote physical health and well-being, and I would recommend the wearing or carrying of one as a protector against rogue cells in the atmosphere;

Rose Quartz is said to help with emotional release and concerns; and Amethyst with spirituality.

The correct music, or sound and vibrational therapy, applied to an off-tune (out of balance) chakra or energy centre, or generally, can also be beneficial and, help to re-balance us. Certain music can very quickly produce mood swings, bringing joy and peace to our ailing spirit within. Conversely, the wrong sort of music, which can vary between individuals, can of course have a reverse influence; with noise pollution: which really needs to be discouraged if not outlawed, becoming a more recognised threat to health.

Music which is often titled *new age music*, can be very therapeutic, helping to calm and relax us, and it is often recommended for those suffering from stress, or having trouble relaxing; again we can find expressions used in our language to reflect the therapeutic value of music, such as *music to calm the soul* and, *music to soothe the savage beast*.

Since we are to a degree *light-beings* vibrating at a certain frequency, it should really be quite obvious to us that colours, crystals, music, and any sound, vibration, or concentrated variation of light, must influence us to some degree; and many orthodox practitioners of medicine now seem to agree with this, while it is only the degree of influence which is the main division between them and complementary therapists. My forecast, which is very likely shared by a great many others, is that all forms of therapy akin to those mentioned in this answer will, in time, be recognised, and will eventually be accepted by mainstream medicine, and ultimately, as greater knowledge and understanding of their applications grow, will themselves become greatly used treatment methods of mainstream medicine. (Books, such as *Gem Therapy* as mentioned in the Bibliography).

43. DO OUR DREAMS HAVE MEANING?

Our night-time dreams fall into two main categories: one physical, and the other spiritual.

Many of our dreams reflect our conscious thoughts, deeds, desires and perhaps more often emotions; and what actually occurs is that all our experiences and reactions are examined by, and stored within, our subconscious minds, often in symbolic form. Thus, for example: our subconscious symbolic interpretation for a romantic emotional upset might be reflected through a scene involving water, and if a severe upset, then our symbolic interpretation can be one of severe flooding, storms at sea, or something similar.

The subconscious mind is spiritual, its function is that of pivot between our higher spirit mind and our physical consciousness, thus it needs to analyse everything that happens to us, and store the information. While it also directs and controls what we often consider automatic functions within our physical body, such as the action of our involuntary muscles, for instance: our heart and stomach, while it also influences the functioning of our endocrine and other bodily glands, so, even during our sleep periods, it is never totally inactive.₁

The subconscious mind not only uses symbols and symbolic images to store, but also to relate information; which incidentally is a method used to communicate information by those on the higher levels of the spirit world, a method of communication which eliminates the use of words which can often have more than one meaning. It is said that communication on the higher levels of the spirit world, using symbolic thought forms, is able to encapsulate the complete meaning of any thought without the possibility of confusion or misunderstanding.

On a spiritual level, our dreams can be divided into two aspects, the first and more common would be similar to the physical aspect already mentioned, but in this case it is memories of spirit world experiences or journeys: for while we sleep a great many of us leave our bodies, and our spirits take journeys into the spirit realms of existence. We do so for two purposes, one: to undertake some form of learning, which might be very different to earthly forms of learning, and secondly: for pleasure, perhaps to meet old friends and relatives. Upon waking we can rarely remember visiting the spirit world in any great detail, if at all, because physical brain is incapable of receiving the complete memory of such journeys; it is like trying to transfer the memory, stored within the world's most sophisticated master computer, into an inferior system, which the brain is, the information either fails to be recorded, or, it is fragmented and scrambled to such an extent it becomes unfathomable. This is partially because our 'out of body' night time journeys might last for several hours, whereas our brains, which might try to capture the spiritual experiences, often only manage to receive distorted versions, and they have been edited to just a few minutes.

The reason why our brains, our conscious minds, fail to receive a version of greater clarity, is because, when we enter what might be described as sleep-mode, the part of the subconscious mind which supplies memory to our conscious minds, also becomes largely inactive, thus nightly experiences which take place in the spirit world are not able to be passed, in any great detail, to the consciousness of our brains.

The other aspect of spiritual consideration is that of *dream messages* and we are all capable of receiving such; for it is often the ideal time for our friends and guides to implant thoughts and ideas within us; additionally, such messages can equally come from our own higher consciousness, that part of ourselves which remains free from the confusion of physical life.

The majority of us simply dismiss our dreams as meaningless, despite the fact that there are a great many recorded cases of prophetic dreams on record, such as the number of people who foretold the sinking of the Titanic. Some people who experience prophetic dreams see a literal scene, while others might receive the same message in symbolic form. Messages received in symbolic form are not transmitted in this format to make it difficult for us to understand, but rather because messages are often difficult for us to remember: therefore the shorter the message--the more chance of us retaining and transferring the memory to the conscious mind.

During dreams, which on a conscious level are mostly forgotten, we perhaps all receive messages, and these are stored within our subconscious minds, where they might register and perhaps remain for some time, although eventually will, in some form, 'filter' into our conscious thoughts, perhaps as a flash of inspiration, and thus influence us at some point in the future.

So our dreams can indeed have great meaning, and can, if we can train ourselves to remember them (keeping a pen and paper by the bed to record them immediately upon waking is highly recommended), be used to guide us.

Occasionally, although rarely, some of us have dreams which reflect past-life experiences, particularly *end of life* traumas which we never fully came to terms with; this is because some aspect of the memory still needs to be released, and until it is, might continue to cause a disturbance at a subconscious level. Sometimes, although again rarely, the dream caused by a past life trauma has even been known to influence and even cause physical marks to manifest during the current incarnation, such as the scars of old knife or bullet wounds. In such cases, beneficial help might be forthcoming in a number of ways, such as: meditation, when one can attempt to gain clearer recall of the trauma, and to release the experience, so that it ceases to be troublesome in the current life. Spiritual healing might also prove effective, for the emotional trauma, and negative energy blockage it might have caused, could be released by its application. Lastly, past life regression, through hypnosis, might also be able to help recall and release the trauma, so that its influence upon the current life is removed.

Such things, and so many links with other levels of consciousness, are dreams made of.

44. WHY DO SO MANY PEOPLE REMEMBER VISITING OTHER REALMS DURING 'NEAR-DEATH EXPERIENCES'?

When someone has an accident, a heart attack, or something similar, the shock often causes their spirit to temporarily leave their physical body; but obviously its connecting link is not completely severed, otherwise they would never be able to return.

Upon return, those who have had a 'near death experience' often report very similar experiences: of entering another dimension, one of light and beauty; and one which many are very reluctant to leave, but either do so involuntarily: when they suddenly find themselves being drawn back into their physical body, or after discussion with guides, friends or relatives they agree to return, and this can be for a whole range of personal reasons.

While sleeping at night we often visit the spirit world, and remember little or nothing of what we have been doing; the reason for this is because the part of our subconscious mind which deals with memory has largely switched to an inactive sleep-mode. Whereas, if we have a 'near death experience', our subconscious mind has not had the opportunity to switch to sleep-mode, and is therefore more actively aware of our spirit's journey into the spirit world.

The experience still has to be transferred to our conscious recollection, but this is possible to a far greater degree, although not necessarily complete, because of the fact our subconscious mind never entered its sleep-mode condition. For our subconscious mind is the *go-between* of our higher spiritual mind and our physical brain, or consciousness. This is also why meditation experiences can generally be remembered far better than dreams, for they also pass through our non-sleeping subconscious mind, as do all spirit communications, such as: clairvoyance and clairaudience.

45. IS MEDITATION ADVISABLE, AND IF SO HOW SHOULD WE MEDITATE?

In its truest sense, the idea of meditation is to bring us closer to the aspect of God within, as well as to the aspect of God we might consider external. To bring peace of mind and self-control, to help us to harmonise mind, body and spirit; all of which will naturally bring us closer to God; and this can also prove beneficial to health, so it is indeed highly advisable.

It is perhaps the finest self-discipline we could develop in life, and a good idea for all to practice. I personally believe it should be taught and practised daily in all schools, for it would help children to relax, and therefore to become more attentive and responsive, and in time this would develop better adults: by helping them become more in harmony with themselves and their true spiritual nature. It is also universal, and should not be considered a 'religious' act, or favouring any one religion.

Meditation can be undertaken singularly or in groups, it can be undertaken in silence, with a guided talk, or with the influence of gentle, pleasant music. There are no set rules, and each of us must find the best approach for ourselves, and not be afraid to change it, if it should become stale.

To begin: we should relax the body, to aid this we can use various methods: such as flexing or contracting our muscles, then releasing the tension. It often helps at the outset to visualise a symbol, or a pleasing scene, perhaps a flower or a garden, or the flame of a candle. The object being to discipline the mind: so that thoughts do not keep wandering onto daily activities; I personally find music helps relaxation, it also creates vibrations of colour, which can assist in self-healing.

Lone meditation is perhaps associated with someone who isolates themselves in a quiet room, sits comfortably with eyes closed, and plays gentle music, for anything from ten to thirty minutes, and perhaps these are the ideal conditions. But with practise, a true aspirant will be able to meditate (even if for the briefest period of time) almost anywhere; on a quiet seat in a park, leaning against a tree, or even while gently strolling. The moment may last for only a few fleeting seconds, but this is all right, for it realises its aim: which is for a closer link to the aspect of God within.

When meditating, the wearing of clothing with relaxing shades of colour is said to help, with pale shades of such as yellow or turquoise ideal, as all colours contain their own vibration, with the vibration of the seven colours of the rainbow matching closely the seven notes of the musical scale; we can begin to appreciate why a relaxing colour (tone or note) is desirable.

Meditation is not necessarily a means of unfolding or developing spiritual gifts, although this can happen if circumstances are right, and we have the right motive at heart. So we should not worry over the expectation of such development, as it may not be within our life-plan. Instead we should seek inner peace, and harmony with the aspect of God within, and with all of creation.

During meditation it is also fine if we slip into such a deep level of relaxation we do not remember much if any of what might have been heard by others (although ideally not actually to be sleeping), for at a higher level of consciousness we will be linked with spirit guides and teachers, and will benefit with some form of learning (probably via the subconscious mind): which will be beneficial to us at a later time. The desire for a closer link with the God within is also a positive assertion, or affirmation, and is therefore a cause which must eventually produce an effect, and one which inevitably will bring spiritual 'reward', and if this is not more obviously forthcoming during our current lifetime, then certainly it will be in the spirit world and during a future incarnation.

46. IS POSITIVE THINKING BENEFICIAL?

Our mind is a creative spiritual faculty which has vast power and potential, as we think we are creating positive or negative energy, causing reverberations, which can, and eventually will, have an effect upon us on all levels of mind, body and spirit.

The outflow of thoughts from our minds effect us in a great many ways, perhaps more noticeably with our health: where positive thinking has been shown to be beneficial. Although what most of us fail to understand or consider: is that every single thought we have is engaging, or drawing to us, the consequences of natural spiritual laws; and these are in continuous operation, and just as we can receive the beneficial effects of positive thinking, we can just as easily receive the undesirable effects of negative thinking. For *ALL* our thoughts, words and deeds create energy, which, eventually, will quite naturally be returned to us; and this is the law of cause and effect, or karma, which is a natural spiritual law, and like all spiritual laws: the consequence of its operation or outworking is inescapable. So it is certainly advisable for each of us to try to think in a positive manner, and of course, not forgetting the words and deeds, to lead what we would term a good life.

Additionally, our thoughts will attract certain people toward us, on the physical level and also from the spirit world, for a natural law of God is that *like attracts like.* If we think good positive thoughts: we will attract like-minded spirit people and helpers, if we think in a negative manner: this will attract equally negative spirit people. This may sound a little worrying or disheartening to anyone who might consider themselves rather too negative, but of course nobody ever thinks in an entirely negative manner at all times, so it is always possible to reverse the effect. We all have personal responsibility, and will eventually, even if it takes many lifetimes, learn through experience.

When we lose a loved one, we should try to remember the positive, considering they are now free from pain and earthly problems, in a much brighter, happier place. If we lose a job, instead of dwelling on the negative: we can think of the new challenges ahead, which will bring greater scope for learning, a chance to meet different people, and make new friends. When we hear of reported tragedies: we can once more remember that nobody ever truly dies, the experiences may not be pleasant, but we cannot judge why they might even have been chosen by those involved; and we rarely consider how others might spiritually gain from their personal experiences.

As mentioned earlier: thinking in a positive manner can also be beneficial to health, for it helps to create harmony on all levels of being: mind, body and spirit. Negative energy can disturb the vibrations of one or more of our finer energy bodies, which can in turn lead to ill-health; and this aspect alone gives us a very good reason to make every effort to develop and make use of our ability to think in a positive manner.

Like all things in life: balance rather than extreme, is desirable; generally I would say we cannot strive too strongly to maintain a positive outlook, for most of us would never take our positive

153

behaviour to the extreme of being foolhardy, and all too many of us slip more easily into a negative mood, so we constantly need to be on personal alert, so that we do not allow the negative side of our personality any opportunity to dominate.

Unfortunately, some people confuse positive thinking, and subsequent behaviour, with zealous determination; they consider that if they pursue an ambition with a *positive* enough attitude they will succeed; confusing positive thinking with personal motivation. The purer positive thinking I am advocating, has very little in common with this type of attitude, which in fact can be very negative; it has more to do with inner spiritual awareness and personal development, for to be a truly balanced and whole person we must not be driven by our ego, merely pursuing the fulfilment of physical desire.

Motive must be right, and ideally we should be engaging our intuition with our positive thinking; for in this way there is far greater chance that the correct motive, and need, of mind, body and spirit, will be considered. If it isn't, the chances are we will merely be considering the fulfilment of our physical desires, which may well be detrimental to ourselves, our spiritual progression and, as is often the outcome, detrimental to others as well. The first rule to apply to ourselves is to question whether our words or deeds, the subsequent actions of our thoughts, are unnecessarily hurtful or harmful to anyone else, if we know they are, then we should consider changing them. Although, particularly with volatile human emotions, there will always be those circumstances when we will not be able to avoid hurting one person or another, and in such cases we can only do what we intuitively feel is right.

Positive thinking, not the misconstrued concept mentioned earlier, if practised, ideally with inner intuitive awareness, will reap many rewards for mind (more relaxed, contented and in control), body (potentially improved health) and spirit (greater progression); making it one of the most important disciplines we could ever master.

47. HOW IMPORTANT IS QUALITY OF LIFE?

True quality of life is very important, without health and happiness most of us would quite rightly consider our life to lack quality; but, in my opinion, we also need to acknowledge our spiritual nature, otherwise I believe true, and certainly deeper quality, will always elude us.

This may appear a rather strange statement, and many might wonder what spiritual acknowledgement has to do with quality of life. My explanation is simple: I believe that the widespread lack of knowledge concerning our spiritual nature leaves many millions of us floundering in the dark, forever seeking, for something which to so many of us is an elusive unknown. That elusive missing stimuli to our lives, preventing peaceful contentment, is our submerged spiritual nature, our true self, trying to gain acknowledgement and fulfilment.

My first point, and perhaps the most important one, is that the true quality of life of which I speak, has little or nothing to do with possessions. Quality of life should most certainly not be equated with material wealth and status, whether we own a big house, a new top of the range car, and expensive electrical luxuries. Far too many people have allowed their material greed to developed beyond all sensible proportion, and they have become mercenary and money orientated to the point where they really no longer own their possessions, and in a sense their possessions own them. For so many are enslaved to possessions through financial debt while they suffer in unhappy, stressful employment, simply so that they can maintain their false quality of life.

The world is currently run with monetary systems, or money markets, and we are all encouraged to grab as big of a share as we can. Money is of course a necessity, to pay for essential supplies and services, but really it is just a convenient form of barter which has grown out of all proportion to its value, and out of control; with the greedy grabbing more, very often to the detriment of others. If only we could all wake from our spiritual sleep, and realise, that life is for spiritual growth; and not as a game of who can accumulate the greatest material wealth.

Many of the greedy also seem to gain a so-called *position* in society, and are treated differently to the average person. Such people are often given knighthood's and other so-called honours, and are held in high esteem; many for 'services' to a number of former state industries, despite the fact such people have, for their employment, already been paid what an average person would consider a fortune.

Each of us could 'die' tomorrow, and find ourselves in the spirit world; what a sad day this could be for so many, when they realise that to have sought material glorification, to the exclusion of spiritual progression, will account for nothing worthy in the spirit world. Such deeds will indeed weigh heavily, particularly where material desire has proven detrimental to others, those who have behaved in such a way will surely have great regret, and much still to learn.

There is of course nothing wrong with money itself, it is a very useful tool, if it is simply used for barter, and not given more importance, power and dominion, than life itself. How any individual or government can put money before the health of someone in need of treatment, is beyond belief. Money is not the root of all evil, it is the manner in which it is used which raises or lowers the consciousness of mankind, and therefore affects the true deeper quality of life, at the spiritual level.

If someone has the knack of acquiring money they have a powerful tool, which they could easily turn to good use; instead of worshipping money, and investing it to produce yet more financial wealth, they could channel it into good causes, such as feeding the hungry, and housing the homeless. Indeed it would be extremely beneficial if more were to be channelled into developing spiritual awareness, with the construction of spiritual teaching and healing centres. For those who find such knowledge and begin to awaken their true spiritual nature, often ask where, and why, this information has been hidden, and denied them all of their life.

Quality of life should improve for all of us, as we begin to understand the true spiritual nature of life. This, of course, will not take away experiences and lessons we are each here to learn from, but it will make it easier to understand why certain experiences are necessary; while also making us more aware of our personal responsibility in the shaping of our eternal destiny.

To have quality in life we all need to be reasonably happy, and to feel of value and use, with the majority needing to have some form of employment. But to give real quality to life, it should be some form of employment which gives job satisfaction, and which we are happy to be engaged in, and at the same time, does not put us under excessive pressure or stress. Job satisfaction being much more important to quality of life than income, which should of course be adequate, and enough to purchase or cover the necessities of life, such as housing, food, clothing, warmth in winter, and of course all the other general bills. Provided this is so, additional income is a bonus, albeit on occasions a welcome one, and vast excess should not be striven for as a necessity, for to do so begins the downfall of spiritual quality.

Health is of obvious importance to quality of life, and it generally breaks down if we fail to maintain a reasonable state of harmony; if the mental or emotional equilibrium of the finer energy bodies becomes unsettled, or if we fail to take reasonable care of our physical bodies; although we can also be unfortunate, and fall victim to such as a virus through physical contact, or to rogue cells in the atmosphere. To help readers to a clearer understanding of what this might mean, I will now take a look at each of the three aspects: mental, emotional and physical; all of which can be disturbed, and adversely affect health and quality of life.

First of all I will look at the mental aspect: mental stress, strain or fear, are the main threats to the balance of the finer mental energy body, and thus to health. As any of these negative reactions register in the finer mental body, they disturb the balance, which in turn is often reflected through the physical body, in the form of ill health. This is because all of the finer energy bodies are linked and inter-connected from the highest through to the physical, therefore what disturbs one, must to some degree disturb all.

For example: and I return to employment, if we are unhappy in our work the stress this can cause, especially if we are not in control of the work-flow, can disturb our finer mental body. This might then work itself through into the physical body, where symptoms could take many forms, maybe a stomach ulcer, perhaps migraine, and if the cause is not alleviated, eventually a heart attack, cancer, blood clots and so forth, the list is endless.

The answer to this particular problem is simple, although these days not necessarily easy to put into practise; it is to find another form of employment, something which satisfies, and in which reasonable control over the work-flow can be exercised. We should not sell our peace of mind and health for a higher income, it is not worth it; we cannot take material wealth with us when we pass, but we DO take our level of spiritual attainment, and in reality this is worth far more than the transient illusions of the material world.

Obviously, it is not only stressful employment which can disturb our finer mental body; so if we are suffering from stress we must first identify its cause, then we can plan which changes we might be able to make to our circumstances to alleviate it. If we find ourselves in a position where, for a time, we are unable to change circumstances to alleviate the stress, to help ourselves we would be well advised to use positive thought, meditation and relaxation techniques. With the positive thought process we can strengthen ourselves against the stress, so that if the problem continues or repeats, it will simply wash over us, as an expected irritation which is largely to be ignored. To achieve this, we should start by considering it in its rightful perspective, by analysing it in comparison with God's majestic and wondrous creation, and considering of how little importance our problem is, compared to our own true spiritual nature, and eternal life. With nothing of a material nature ever really worthy of worry or fear, to an infinite spiritual being.

Meditation and relaxation can also be very beneficial in helping to relieve, or reduce mental stress; undertaken with some gentle background music it can calm the nerves, and thus give us more control, so that we are better able to cope. This can of course be linked with positive thinking, when affirmations can be said, reminding us not to become upset or stressed by experiences. Prayer can also help at this time, there is nothing wrong with asking for help and strength to withstand the pressures of life.

Next I come to emotional imbalance, and once again this will disturb our finer (emotional) energy body, then often manifest within the physical, as ill health; here though, the problems which can disturb the emotional energy body can vary greatly. Again, if we are suffering in this way we will need to try and understand, and analyse, why our relationships and dealings with others are disturbing us, and unfortunately this can be very difficult to do. For when we are in the middle of an emotional situation it can be rather difficult to think in a clear and rational way.

However, forewarned is forearmed, and now we are more aware that negative emotional reactions can cause ill health, we should be much more conscious of our responses and reactions, and thus, when appropriate, ready to control emotions in a positive manner. If we are prone to suffer because of our emotions we really need to come to terms with them, to control them to some degree, and not let *them* control us, but not to the point of stifling them, as this can be just as bad as letting them run wild, and in some cases worse. We will need to be able to analyse our emotions, so we can understand why we react as we do, so that we are able to keep a check of them when necessary, and thus stay more in control.

Understanding that emotional upsets can be detrimental to our health may not always make it possible for us to control them, but should help us to more quickly analyse what is disturbing us, giving us more opportunity to correct the situation, at least to some degree, and thus reduce the effect. Talking things over with a good friend can help, but it really must be a good trustworthy friend, not someone who is likely to use our innermost thoughts and feelings as a good source for gossip, otherwise we will probably finish even worse off.

If an emotional imbalance is proving detrimental to our health, we will need to identify its cause, to give us a starting point for sorting out the problem. For example: if our emotional balance is disturbed because of an argument or disagreement, we can try to sort out the problem amicably, remembering once more, that very little is worthy of such disturbance, to an infinite spiritual being. If we are suffering from an emotional imbalance we will need to get in touch with our true inner feelings; if we wish, we can then use the power of prayer to help the situation. With emotional problems meditation, relaxation and positive thinking, will again help, but here I think the power of prayer is even more valuable. For what has generally happened: is that we have allowed another person, in some cases without them even realising, to disturb or upset our emotional balance. To help ourselves, we first need to put the upset into its true perspective, in relation to God's creation, then to be able to forgive the other person involved, from the heart. When ready to do this, through prayer we can ask for healing to be sent to the other person, and for their forgiveness. Provided this is done with true honesty and sincerity, it will almost certainly reduce the emotional imbalance, as well as helping to correct any imbalance the other person might be suffering with.

If our emotional imbalance does not involve another person, we can still help ourselves. To do so, we will still need to be able to analyse the reason for the upset, and to be able to put the situation into a realistic perspective. Having done this, through prayer we can gain help, by acknowledging that our reaction was unworthy, and accepting it was wrong. In this way we will have acknowledged where we were in error, confirming we have learned from our mistake, and this will help toward the re-balancing of the emotional energy body, and in turn benefit health. We can then work on controlling our emotional reactions, strengthening ourselves, so that in future we do not allow our emotions such undisciplined sway, and so easily upset our health and well-being.

Next, I come to the physical body, and our direct effect upon it, through intake and injury. It is commonly known and accepted that excessive food or drink can lead to physical problems; eating too much red meat, fatty foods, products with high sugar content, all can lead to blockages in the veins and arteries, to be followed by heart attacks, and many other complaints. But without a doubt the most destructive of needlessly self-inflicted intakes, commonly consumed today, are the toxins inhaled through the act of cigarette smoking. The damage that is being inflicted because of this habit is nearly endless: asthma, bronchitis, lung infections, pneumonia, cancer, heart disease and failure, and so many more. The damage it can do to others: through passive smoking, is at last gaining more recognition, and the fact that this is still so freely permitted in many public places is very disheartening.

There are thousands of cases each year where parents who smoke damage the health of their babies and children. If we choose to damage ourselves this is bad enough, but inflicting it on others, especially youngsters who are not in a position to complain, is totally unfair. I believe that in perhaps another fifty years, and hopefully much sooner, the habit will have largely disappeared, and future generations will then regard it as a mystery how mankind could have so easily been led into such an unhealthy habit.

I, of course, understand that there are few amongst us who do not have one weakness or another, and that the habit of smoking originally developed with ignorance to its harm, but the truth of how damaging smoking is, has been known for many years now, so it really is time for everyone to take personal responsibility; we are each in charge and control of our actions, and cannot blame others if our quality of life suffers through our own lack of discipline. We should also consider our potential karmic debts, those with children have responsibility toward them, they do not own them, and they do not have the right to inflict potential damage upon them. Another point some might take time to consider, of which I was made aware by a friend who was 'dying' with cancer, is that he once told me that during his time in hospital he had seen that convalescent smokers physically suffered much more than non-smokers, and that they were considerably less likely to recover from surgery.

Injury is often not the fault of the victim, but in a number of cases is due to carelessness, for example: in such a case where serious injury is caused by car or motorcycle accident. Once more self-control and discipline is needed, if we are in control of a vehicle we should observe and obey the rules of the road, travelling below the speed limit, for so many accidents are due to excessive speed. We have personal responsibility for ourselves, but if we injure someone else, through deliberate or careless neglect, we will incur a karmic debt, and that is something we should make every effort to avoid.

For a final summing-up on this quality of life question, I would start by reminding readers that we are first and foremost spiritual beings; and as such: should be living life with this fact considered with every thought, word and deed of life. We would be well advised not to blindly, and without consideration for others, strive for physical luxuries and wealth, but if wealth should come our way, to use it wisely. Instead, I would suggest we strive for harmony in all our thoughts, words and deeds, and in all our relationships. To live life as we would have wished as children, expressing and sharing love with all. To help others, with fair reason to our own needs, while we strive for happiness. Then we will find true quality of life, and when we return to the spirit world we will realise how wise we have been.

Chapter Seven

OPENING THE MIND

Questions 48-50

==

48. WE ARE TOLD MANKIND IS DESTROYING PLANET
EARTH, IS THERE ANY WAY IN WHICH WE CAN HELP
TO HEAL THE WORLD?

There are many ways in which each of us can help repair the
damage which has been inflicted upon this planet by mankind.
Help can be given on both physical and spiritual levels, and each
can range from simple yet practical everyday considerations, to
the more actively involved.

On the physical level we can give simple yet practical help to
the environment, and in some cases to the less privileged, by
recycling whenever possible; with some of the more obvious
items being paper, bottles, cans, clothing and fabrics. We can
also help when making a purchase, by using as many products
as possible where recycling has been applied, and by not
purchasing items which are non-biodegradable.

Energy conservation is another way in which we can all help,
by giving consideration to areas in our home and work where
less energy could be used; the use of lead-free petrol can also
help, and the purchasing of ozone friendly products.
Additionally, if we practise gardening or grow our own
vegetables, organic products would be more environmentally
friendly. When purchasing vegetables if the demand for organic

increased, the farmers and producers would be encouraged to take heed and cater for demand.

Individually, these measures may not appear to be of great significance, but if, in time, enough of us were to respond to the call for such action, understanding how important it is, the collective difference and effect upon the planet and its environment would be enormous.

For those who wish to be more active, in addition to the brief suggestions already given, the joining of environmental groups and organisations such as *Greenpeace* and *Friends of the Earth* is a good practical way of becoming involved. While their literature helps to keep people better informed of what needs to be done, and more aware of any progress being made; information which is rarely covered in the newspapers or by other media.

Our actions can also take the form of lobbying producers, manufacturers and politicians, this is of course being undertaken by such organisations as already mentioned, but each voice which adds to the demand can make the difference between consideration and real change.

The destruction of rain-forests needs to stop, and no tree anywhere in the world should be cut down without a replacement being planted, and because of the destruction already carried out, we need an urgent global replanting project. Again, each of us with a garden can help, by planting our own tree.

Countries with rain-forests should be given the international support they often need, so they do not have to destroy their environment to generate income. The way things are at present many are left with little choice, for it is one of the few ways in which they can survive. They, and those who exploit them, have to be taught that the rain-forests are there to give oxygen to the entire planet, and without them we all suffer, as too does the earth spirit. At the same time the countries with comparatively vast wealth must learn to share their resources, eliminating the others need to destroy.

One of the causation factors which has brought this problem upon us is the Western system of materialism, although the West is not entirely to blame, for many countries around the globe add to the problem because of either their own greed or misdirected finances, all too often handled with a total lack of genuine concern for the majority of the people and the planet as a whole. We all have to learn it is not the way in which eternal spiritual beings should be conducting our earthly lives. Again, as individuals we can help, by joining groups to lobby politicians, if enough of us rebel against the system in, of course, a non-violent manner, then the system will change. Politicians are meant to be in service to all of us, not just to the rich business people, sometimes they need reminding of this fact.

On a spiritual level: we can also help to heal the world, and all the better if combined with the physical considerations. Spiritually, we can actively help by encouraging others to read this book, and numerous other books dealing with the reality of eternal life and spiritual laws, truth and wisdom. Then whenever possible to go further, to seek personal proof, for proof cannot truly be given in any book, what can be given are explanations to the meanings and consequences of such proof.

Spreading spiritual wisdom will in time help the world, for with knowledge comes an awakening to the personal responsibility we each carry, and with the understanding that no person truly dies, and that each must make good for any wrong they do, this truth will help to inspire a response from a great number of people, not through fear, but out of the goodness of their heart; for they will understand their true spiritual heritage. For underneath the materialistic attitude of many is the goodness of the spirit within, it might be misled for a while, and buried deeply, but eventually it rises up and proclaims itself for the glorious spirit and aspect of God it has always been. If we can help teach this truth to just one other person, the knock-on effect will benefit many, many thousands, and eventually millions, and each will be helping to forge a new and more enlightened age.

On an individual spiritual level we can all help without even leaving home, even if bedridden. Since prayers for absent healing to be administered can be requested by anyone, indeed such an act can even prove beneficial to the one making the request, so the benefit can be two-way. The request for healing to be administered does not necessarily have to come from any recognised healing channel, we can all play a part and, in this way, help. We can also request that absent healing energies be sent to help politicians, and others in positions of power, to help them make the right decisions. This may sound fanciful, if not considered with spiritual understanding; it is really a question of sending love, if love is sent and received, in time the receiver might be moved to respond; for it carries a quickening vibration, potentially lifting their spirit to greater awareness, compassion and goodness. This is why spiritual masters teach us to love our enemies, for our love can mellow them, and might bring a change of attitude and mind; therefore to send absent healing energies, is to send vibrations of love. As well as praying for those we personally know to be in need, prayers can be said for the earth-spirit, who is a living being.

To illuminate upon this fact and hopefully inspire each reader to further consideration and greater effort, I transgress slightly to quote a little more from the work of Geoffrey Hodson. In his book *The Kingdom of the Gods*, the author, (who tends to call many of the angels *Gods*) claims to have clairvoyantly seen and communicated with many angelic life forms, and in his book he describes a communication from one such life form, whom he calls a *mountain God*, and this is what the *mountain God* reportedly said about this planet:[1]

"The globe is a living being with incarnate power, life and consciousness. The Earth breathes. Its heart beats. It is the body of a God who is the Spirit of the Earth. Rivers are as its nerves, oceans great nerve-centres. Mountains are the denser structure of the giant whose outer form is man's evolutionary field, whose inner life and potent energies are the abiding place of the Gods."

49. IS THERE LIFE ON OTHER PLANETS?

All of creation contains life, and life in some form, even if undetectable to us, exists on all planets. Furthermore: the very planets themselves are life forms, and should therefore be treated with respect, and loving care. But when considering the question in terms of other planetary beings: every year there are many thousands of reported UFO sightings, from all around the world, and I believe this to be a gentle form of communication, gradually allowing mankind to become aware of and, to accept, other planetary beings.

I do not believe that the vast majority of life forms who come to observe us should in any way be feared, but the fact that through ignorance, if they were to land in an open manner, we might panic, does, I believe, prevent their landing at this present moment in time.

Through such inspired films as *Close Encounters* and *ET*, people are beginning to accept that such beings could be friendly, and need not be feared. When enough of us upon this planet are ready, and can accept their arrival without fear, I believe they will come, and that they will help humanity into a much more fruitful age. In fact, I believe and understand, that other planetary beings did come to this planet many thousands of years ago; not just to visit, but also to create a new life for themselves, and to bring knowledge and understanding to the inhabitants who were already upon earth.

Those other planetary beings, who inhabited a number of areas around the planet, and were originally considered to be Gods, brought greater knowledge of the universe, along with what to our ancestors would have been many new ideas and inventions; many of which have unfortunately been lost. I believe Astrology and Astronomy owe their origins to the influence of such beings, who I understand taught many new concepts and were, at that time, responsible for what must have been a great leap forward in evolution. The planetary beings mixed with the human population, which also makes it highly likely that many of us are, to a now small degree, descended from extra terrestrial beings.

For those who might find this knowledge difficult to accept, I would ask them to imagine the omnipotent power of God, the supreme motivating force within all energy. Since God is the creator of all life, and not just life upon earth, it really is inconceivable, and perhaps conceited, for anyone to imagine that conscious life would only have been seeded upon earth. I further believe those planetary beings who first came to earth did so with the guidance and blessing of spiritual masters.

Truly accepting God as the power which motivates all life makes the concept of other planetary beings easier to assimilate, and spiritual teaching does make it quite clear that God created many life forms, other than mankind. When we can accept angels, nature spirits, and a spirit world where eternal life is lived, all created through the power of God, accepting the concept of life other than human, is really only a small additional step to take. Also, since all life comes from, and is an aspect of God, we must accept that in essence we, and all other planetary beings, are spiritually related beings.

I hope that having reached this page, each reader will (if they did not before), have accepted that their own true status is one of an infinite spiritual being, who temporarily inhabits a physical body, as a vehicle which allows them the opportunity to learn through physical experience. In the same way they might have experienced incarnations on many, and perhaps hundreds of previous occasions, during their eternal existence. What may not be realised, is the fact we might have undertaken similar experiences, and incarnations, upon planets other than earth. In fact, it is very likely that many of us will have previously lived upon one or more other planets, and that we will do so again, at some time in our future. I have personally been told by a guide, speaking through an entranced medium, that I have lived upon at least one other planet during my conscious existence. Added to this, in a development circle I used to attend, I was informed that other planetary beings where present, and I look forward to learning more about them, and perhaps sharing what I discover with readers in some future book.

Before anyone dismisses this information as too unbelievable, let me ask them to think again of the fact we are all infinite spiritual beings, who in one sense have always existed, is the possibility in the expanse of the limitless time-span of eternity so unlikely? And if so, what did we all do before the creation of planet earth? For spiritual beings have always existed, long before this planet was created.

Returning our thought to those we might at present call *Extra Terrestrials*, whom I would rather call our friends from other planets, I can foresee them helping mankind in many ways, such as with what we would consider new inventions. Often the inventions and discoveries of mankind are of a simple nature, almost the obvious, that for some reason had never been tried, or had somehow before been overlooked. We can only imagine how many other inventions and discoveries our friends from the other planets might have made, even if thinking in only a slightly different way to ourselves. For often I think we are stuck in a certain mode of thought; those free from this mode might see and view things with an alternative perspective, while they might also have a greater understanding of universal energies and the natural laws of God, so who knows what improvements they might bring.

With our planet at present being eaten away by pollution and destruction, which the greedy conglomerates and big business empires of the world encourage, by their refusal to change their highest possible profit first policies, I for one welcome any help we can get. I firmly believe one simple and safe form of energy which is available to us right now, is for some reason being overlooked, and this I believe is connected to the magnetic or gravitational pull of the planet herself. With a potentially vast and unlimited reservoir of safe, pure and clean energy available

172

equally all around the planet, if this can be converted to usable energy, it could almost overnight change the physical quality of life for millions upon this planet (hopefully giving them more time to consider their spiritual nature), while helping the planet herself, by alleviating such vast waste, and the pollution it causes. If any reader has a more technical interest in the subject of 'free-energy', in particular a system of utilising the earth's electrical fields to provide a replacement for fossil fuels, Alfred Perry, President of the Energy Science & Technology Corporation would like to hear from them. (See Addresses).

Finally, once again I say, I will welcome the arrival of our friends from other planets, and I further believe they will come, and be known to all, within the next thirty years, and hopefully much sooner.

50. IS GOD A BEING & IS THERE A PURPOSE TO CREATION?

God is the omnipresent, omnipotent, omniscient (ever-present, all-powerful, all-knowing) being of whom all creation is composed or an aspect of; the perfect conscious living mind, present within and a part of all energy; forever finding expression in the wonder of its own creation, producing and developing new forms of life and new aspects of individualised consciousness.

God is not a being living and existing separate from creation, separate from mankind, from flowers and trees, from planets and stars; God exists within all of these things, within all of creation, within all that has ever been, and God will exist within all that ever will be. So God is not a being like ourselves, and

173

does not exist exclusively in human or in any other individual form, for the form of God is creation; indeed, the sum total of all creation, all that exists, is the form of God. While it can also be said that everything that exists does so within the form and consciousness of God. So, God is a being---the *One* being--- while we are merely facets, like individualised cells, within the One being; just as all the cells of the human body make the One person, so all beings, and all within creation, on a multitude of dimensions, constitutes the form of One supreme being. So God is a being of such magnitude and unimaginable vastness that full analysis of this realisation is almost entirely beyond our true comprehension. Therefore mankind, all people, since we are composed of the same energy, are living aspects of God, as are all animals, and all in nature.

It is also fair to say that God is not a being who consciously directs every sequence or repercussion of creation, for much of this is left to what are often described as the natural laws of God, which are not laws which God sat down and pondered over before placing into operation. So should not be confused with fables like the one where Moses supposedly collected the ten commandments of God, for natural laws are not ideals, suggestions or commandments. Nonetheless they are *laws*, for want of a better word, which unlike earth laws are inescapable in their outworking and consequence.

They are called natural laws because they exist and apply themselves quite naturally, they neither require mankind nor spirit world judges---albeit that if there were such they would be potentially highly evolved ones---nor any interference, action, commandment or judgment from God to bring them into operation. They are a natural consequence of our thoughts, words and deeds. The only one of which really needs to be remembered, and considered in all dealings of life, is the law of cause and effect.

One might ask why natural laws exist in the first place, and the answer is because we are all aspects of God, God is perfection, and the aspect of God within all life naturally seeks and is drawn toward this same perfection, desiring to attain to a level of perfection. Natural laws did not therefore need to be placed into operation by decree of God, they always existed, indeed they are what the word implies: *natural*; and in a sense: God is the law and the law is God.

Since we would rightly consider God, *The Supreme Being*, as perfection, we might ponder to consider why life forms were ever created, indeed, whether there is a purpose to creation.

By what I understand, there certainly is a purpose to creation, otherwise we would not exist. Although, the purpose to creation, and our part within may, at first glance, seem to undermine the omniscient perfection we accredit God. For I believe that the fundamental reason for creation, why God created life, in the sense that we might understand and appreciate this, although this may not be anything like the full story, was to learn through the experiences of the different facets or aspects of creation.

This, as I have said, does imply that God is not all-knowing which, in the sense of experience of that which has never happened, seems to me to be a correct analysis. For God can only be all-knowing of that which has happened, that which has been experienced. Although, the infinite experience of God should mean that all potentialities should be calculable to near infinitesimal degree; therefore God must be capable of foreseeing pretty well all eventualities; although to God, as it would be us, I'm sure that this is by no means as satisfactory as actually experiencing them. Hence the thought is put into motion, given energy, so that the outcome can be experienced.

It can therefore be concluded that creation---and all that this entails or causes---is one vast experience undertaken by God; and that God irrefutably knows that every individual facet will seek, however slowly, to achieve perfection through a countless myriad of experiences.

God is of course omniscient in the sense that all knowledge, everything we or any other life form learns or experiences, is instantaneously within the awareness or consciousness of God, for we are all part of God, therefore whatever we learn or experience God also learns and experiences; indeed, our minds are merely aspects of the One mind, so we can never deny the Whole that which we attain. Therefore, God must forever possess all knowledge that is or has ever been accumulated.

So there we have it, in a sense, God is a being who, despite possessing infinite wisdom, partially, perhaps even largely, accumulated through the experiences of the infinite variety and expressions of life, on many dimensions of existence, still, through the experiences of the parts, seeks to become wiser. This, if one is needed, is God's never-ending motivation for infinite existence; and since we are all aspects of God, it is also the root of our own desire, to become wiser, and through personal experience, to move closer to and be more God like. We can hinder and slow our progression, but ultimately, it is within and a part of who and what we are, the deep seated desire and motivation of our spirit, so in time it will draw us onward and ever upward toward perfection.

If anyone has trouble understanding or comprehending the complexities that this question and answer can conjure, do not worry, for it is an hypothesis that could be expanded and expounded to fill many volumes. Suffice it to say, that the grandeur of creation, what lies ahead to learn, and our ability to comprehend can and surely will---if we have made such a spiritual quest part of our lives---continue to be occupied for countless years to come; and even then, we might only have scratched the surface of all that lies ahead of us, to be absorbed over aeons of earthly time.

SUMMARY & FINAL THOUGHTS

===

In the foreword of this book, I said my wish was to provide readers with simple, easy to understand answers; I hope and trust that I have been successful, and that although this book may appear moderate in its number of pages, it will have seemed large in content. I have covered the basic questions asked by seekers of such knowledge and, in some places, gone a little further, into areas which might have been of concern, and certainly of interest. My hope and greatest wish is that all readers, having reached this page, will by now (if they did not before), accept and feel confident in the fact they will survive 'death', with eternal life guaranteed to follow.

There is another way of describing the process which occurs at 'death', which is easy to remember, and especially helpful when dealing with children, for it is simple, yet pleasing to the mind. This is to imagine the beautiful Butterfly, emerging from the chrysalis of the Caterpillar, we would not say the Caterpillar had died, rather that it had transformed into a more beautiful creature. In a similar way, each one of us will one day leave our physical body behind, and emerge as the beautiful spirit we, in reality, have always been. Those remaining upon earth will not (unless suitably clairvoyant) be able to see us, for we will be vibrating at a frequency out of their sensory range, but we will nonetheless have emerged to a new, better and more glorious life.

I further hope and trust that this book will have opened readers minds to the greater realities and possibilities which surround us all, to a greater understanding of natural laws, while also stimulating the imagination. My answers have explained how guides and angels are regularly with each of us, and indeed will it not be wonderful to meet them upon passing? I have also related the importance of personal responsibility, in its many guises, and said how karma will take effect, for there is no escape from the consequences of our thoughts, words and deeds, whether they be good or bad. I have also mentioned how eternal progress is open to each of us, even the seemingly lowest, and those who might be labelled evil. I also hope my comments on health and quality of life will have been of interest and value.

I have also given my thoughts concerning life on other planets, and possible future developments. Some aspects may at present seem strange and impossible, but if we can keep an open mind, never dismissing any possibility, we will allow ourselves much greater scope and potential for personal growth and spiritual progress; for I believe there are many more secrets of life to be unfolded for humanity, in the years to follow this century.

I have titled this *Summary and Final Thoughts*, but for those readers who have further questions, to which they have trouble finding answers, they need not regard these as my final thoughts. For if they wish, they can write to me, via the same address as given for Absent healing, and I will gladly do my best to answer additional questions. To close: I would ask each reader to continually keep an open mind, for I do not believe that even the writers of the finest science fiction have delved deeply enough into their imaginations, to touch upon what the future may hold for all of us upon this planet.

Finally, may God's love be with all readers, and my special best wishes go to all who plan to devote more of their life to research, investigation and spiritual service; may they find greater understanding of spiritual knowledge, truth and wisdom.

BRIEF GLOSSARY OF TERMS

==

* *ANGELS*: Are beings from a line of evolution different to the human form, while they do not incarnate in human form, on occasions, such as: *healing* they help the human form. They also oversee nature and nature spirits, and assist life on earth in its many forms, and in a variety of ways.

* *APPORTS*: The materialisation of physical objects such as coins, historic relics, jewellery and flowers.

* *ASPORTS*: The dematerialisation of physical objects, such as listed under Apports.

* *ASTRAL PROJECTION*: The ability to leave the physical body and travel anywhere upon earth, or as far as the astral plane of existence. The astral plane being the first spirit world plane between the earth and the higher levels of the spirit world. Some people can achieve Astral Projection while in meditation, but the majority who experience it do so while they sleep.

* *AURA*: The electromagnetic energy field, etheric and other finer energy bodies, which surround and inter-connect from the highest through to the physical body. Sometimes partially, and more rarely fully, visible to those with clairvoyant vision.

* *CHAKRAS*: There are seven main chakras which link through the etheric body with the physical body (plus a further two--and perhaps four more other than these, with higher purpose), and these can also be referred to as energy or psychic centres. The chakras are links or vortices within the etheric and other finer energy bodies, through which various energies, including communication, can flow to, and from, the physical body. They

are located approximately at the base of the spine, the spleen, the solar plexus, the heart, the throat, the brow, and at the crown of the head. While a further two main chakras which do not connect directly with the physical body are located one above the crown and one below the base, with as many as four further chakras associated with higher spiritual aspects of our being.

* *CLAIRAUDIENCE.* (Objective): The ability to hear spirit world communicators as though their voices are coming from external sources, in a similar manner to normal hearing.

* *CLAIRAUDIENCE.* (Subjective): The ability to hear spirit world communicators as though their voices, or thoughts, are manifesting directly inside the head.

* *CLAIRSENTIENCE.* (Objective and Subjective): The ability to feel spirit impressions, such as pain previously suffered by a spirit world communicator.

* *CLAIRVOYANCE.* (Objective): The ability to see spirit world communicators as though external to the physical body, in a similar manner to normal vision, but sometimes with their appearance seeming less solid.

* *CLAIRVOYANCE.* (Subjective): The ability to see spirit world communicators through internal vision, using what is often described as the third eye, which creates a picture inside the forehead by way of the brow chakra.

* *DEATH*: 'Death' is merely a transition, from one frequency of vibration where it is necessary to use a physical body to function, to another frequency or level where the spiritual body is used to live a continuous and potentially happy life.

* *DESTINY*: The outworking of plans made before birth which, if an individual follows inner direction (intuition), will be likely to come to fruition. If inner direction is not followed destiny, or

pre-birth plans, will be much less likely to unfold as would be desired upon a higher level of consciousness.

* *DIRECT VOICE*: The physical phenomena of audible spirit world voices, usually speaking through a trumpet.

* *EARTHBOUND*: A spirit person who is bound to the earth, perhaps by desire, or through lack of understanding, such as not accepting their physical passing or, deliberately wishing to stay close to the earth. Perhaps to remain close to a particular person, or desiring to remain within or near to a particular building. A spirit person can also be temporarily earthbound if they suffer an unexpected or sudden shock, through their manner of passing. Such as in a violent passing through accident, murder, suicide or war.

* *EARTH SPIRIT*: Like all forms of physical matter, which can only exist with the presence of spirit energy, and disintegrate or dissolve when the spirit energy departs, the earth planet herself is a living being.

* *ECTOPLASM*: A material or substance which, usually during a physical circle or demonstration, is extracted from or through a Physical medium, while a little can also be extracted from other sitters, which can be moulded or built, to form such as a partial or fully materialised spirit world person. Upon conclusion, the ectoplasm being returned to the medium and other sitters.

* *ETHERIC*: A subtle body of energy which surrounds and connects individually with each person, and the planet. A part of which is an emanation from the physical body.

* *ELECTRONIC VOICE PHENOMENA* (EVP): Is the audible taped recorded voices of spirit world communicators, impressed directly upon an otherwise blank cassette tape while in a

machine which is set to record, with the voices not otherwise heard until the tape is replayed.

* *FINER ENERGY BODIES* (or subtle bodies): We all have a number of finer energy bodies which can sometimes be seen by clairvoyants, in the form of an aura around the physical body. These bodies are referred to under various names, such as *etheric, emotional, mental,* and *higher-self.* There are seven which link with the physical body via the chakras, while a further two are believed to be in the etheric, and as many as four others (higher aspect bodies), making thirteen in total, might actually exist.

* *FREE-WILL:* At all times the human spirit has free-will, or personal responsibility, although at times this may not seem so, since fate often seems to indicate a predetermined destiny. Even on the extremely rare occasions when events do seem to defy free-will, I am certain that it is ourselves making decisions on our higher level of consciousness.

* *GOD:* Is the omnipresent, omnipotent, omniscient being of whom all creation is composed or an aspect of; the perfect conscious living mind, present within and a part of all energy; forever finding expression in the wonder of its own creation, producing and developing new forms of life and new aspects of individualised consciousness.

* *GUIDES* (or spirit guides): Are those who try to help and teach us from the spirit world, with at least one remaining with, or in close association with each of us, throughout our entire incarnation.

* *HELL:* The name given to the lower, or lowest level of the spirit world. Where it is wrongly believed people who were evil, wicked, cruel, sinful, or unworthy in some way, are condemned to spend eternity. Spiritual teachings tell us that the lower levels

are not pleasant, but nobody is trapped within them forever, when they are ready and willing all are free to learn and thus to progress to finer and higher levels.

* *HIGHER-SELF* (or Higher-Mind): We each have a higher consciousness which remains largely free, or independent (above), from our physical body and lower mental thoughts, while through our intuition, conscience, and subconscious mind, it attempts to direct us onto the best pathway for our personal spiritual growth and development.

* *INDEPENDENT DIRECT VOICE*: The physical phenomena of audible spirit world communicators, heard speaking from seemingly mid-air by all present, through a spirit world created ectoplasmic or new energy voice box.

* *INCARNATION*: Life through a physical body.

* *INSTRUMENTAL TRANSCOMMUNICATION* (ITC): Is a growing form of communication being received world-wide from spirit world communicators, who are making use of modern technology. With messages being received over or through such as radios, computers, fax machines, video images, and the telephone.

* *KARMA*: The law of cause and effect. Which is a natural spiritual law, which dictates that whatsoever we do or cause, will have an effect which will rebound or reverberate to us. Either in the current life, in the spirit world, or perhaps in a future incarnation.

* *LEVITATION*: The raising of objects, or people, by spirit world communicators.

* *MATERIALISATION*: The partial or full materialisation of spirit world people, traditionally constructed out of ectoplasm, although in some circles new energy is currently being used to achieve this phenomena.

184

* *MEDIUM*: A spiritual medium forms the link between those who wish to communicate, or convey energies, from the spirit world, to those upon earth. Mediumship can take many forms, including clairvoyance, clairaudience, clairsentience, physical, psychic art, and healing.

* *PHYSICAL PHENOMENA*: The direct physical evidence of spirit world communication, through such as materialisation, direct voice (either through a trumpet or independently), levitation, telekinesis, transfiguration, apports and asports.

* *PSYCHIC ART* (or Spiritual art): This usually takes the form of portrait drawings of those living in the spirit world, which are produced by a medium known as a psychic or spiritual artist; who works under direction or inspiration, and may see, feel or hear the communicating spirit, or be overshadowed, so that their hand is partially directed by the person whose portrait is being drawn.

* *PSYCHOMETRY*: The ability, through psychic or auric senses to receive impressions relating to another person, usually achieved by handling something, such as an object, which has been held or worn by the other person.

* *REINCARNATION*: Re-birth, as a baby, into another physical body. The incarnating ego having formed a link with the new life form since conception.

* *SEANCE*: A meeting, usually a circle of people, seeking communication with those from the spirit world.

* *SIN*: Considered by orthodox religion to be an offence against moral or religious law or divine commandments. Whereas, I would suggest that as well as those crimes which are a moral offence, sin is equally an act which causes disharmony to the transgressor.

* *SOUL*: The finer energy body, or form, which the spirit manifests through, which is linked to the physical body, through other finer energy bodies. The soul body, can also be called the celestial, heavenly or spiritual body, and is the highest aspect of the permanent and eternal body used in the spirit world upon passing. Having taken with it, substance and all relative information contained in all other finer energy bodies.

* *SPIRIT*: The essence which motivates all life, a spark from and a part of the divine mind of God.

* *SPIRIT REALMS* (Levels or Spheres): Are various levels of the spirit world, where life distinct from the physical exists. The realm one progresses to live upon, being the consequence of one's level of spiritual progression or attainment.

* *SPIRITUAL HEALING*: A spiritual healing medium, is a link person between spirit world healers, guides, and angels of healing; who is able to channel remedial spirit energies, through (in broad terms) their own spirit, to the spirit of another, to effect improvement in the health of mind, body or spirit. The resultant spiritual healing energies bringing balance to the finer energy bodies, chakras, and subsequently (if needed), usually through glands and organs via meridian pathways, to the physical body.

* *SPIRIT WORLD* (Heaven): Is another dimension, consisting of many levels, realms or spheres, to which we return upon 'death'.

* *TELEKINESIS*: The movement of objects, usually by spirit world communicators.

* *TRANSFIGURATION*: The ectoplasmic or new energy build-up of a spirit world face, over the face of a medium, for the purpose of recognition, as proof of continued existence.

APPENDIX

==

I am not generally someone who likes written prayers, for I believe that whenever possible our prayers should come from within, from the heart, expressing our innermost thoughts and feelings, and where there is a genuine need, such as for healing, our prayers should reflect this.

However, as I came to complete this book, I was inspired to remember and include for all to share, a beautiful prayer called *Teach Me To Love*. I do not know anything of the original author, but I thank him or her, because it says so much of what I too feel. While it is also what so many upon this planet need to develop more deeply within; for if, to a sufficient degree we can all do so, all we could ever wish for in life will, in time, quite naturally follow.

TEACH ME TO LOVE

There was a time, when in my daily prayer, I asked for all the things I deemed most fair and necessary to my life, success, riches of course, and ease and happiness, a host of friends, a home without alloy, a primrose path of happiness and joy. Ambition ruled my way, I longed to do great things that all my little world might view, and whisper, wonderful.

Oh, Great Spirit, how blind we are, until through natural law you lead us on to better things; today I have but one partition, Great Spirit, teach me to love. Indeed it is my greatest and my only need. Teach me to love not those who first loved me, but all the world, with that rare purity of broad outstretching thought, that bears no trace of earthly taint, but holds in its embrace, humanity, and seems to see, only the good in all, reflected, Great Spirit, from thee.

Teach me, Great Spirit, how to love the most, those who stand most in need of love, that host of people who are poor and sick and bad, whose tired faces show their lives are sad. Who toil along life's way, with footsteps slow, and hearts more heavy than the world can know. People who modest pass discreetly by, and fail to hear the pleading and the cry for help, amongst the tumult of the crowd. People whose anguish makes them cold and proud, bitter, resentful, sullen in their grief.

I long to bring them comfort and relief, to put my hand in theirs, and at their side walk softly on. Oh faithful, fearless guide, ever near, help me to find those lost ones, doubly dear, because they need so much. Help me to seek and find that which they thought was lost, to speak such words of cheer, that as we pass along, the wilderness will burst forth into song.

Oh love divine, how empty was that prayer of other years, at which was once so fair, those empty baubles that the world calls joys, have nothing to me now, but broken toys, outlived, outgrown. I thank thee that I know those much desired dreams of long ago, like Butterflies have had their summer day of brief enchantment, and have gone; today, I pray for better things, thou knowest, Great Spirit, my one desire now....teach me to love.

NOTES

About The Author
1. *Leonard, Maurice, The Medium*: The Biography of Jessie Nason, (London: Regency Press Ltd., 1974) p. 102.

Question 11
1. Hodson, Geoffrey, *The Kingdom of the Gods*, (Madras & London: Theosophical Publishing House, 1987) p. 165.

Question 17
1. Cox, Peter, *The New Why You Don't Need Meat*, (London: Bloomsbury Publishing Ltd., 1992) p. 30.
2. Ibid., p. 27.
3. Ibid., pp. 2-9.

Question 24
1. Ortzen, Tony, Ed., *The Seed of Truth*, (London: Psychic Press Ltd., 1987) p. 165.
2. Ibid., pp. 166-7.

Question 28
1. Foy, Robin, P., *In Pursuit of Physical Mediumship*, (London: Janus Publishing Company, 1996) p. 298.
2. Ibid., p. 306.

Question 32
1. Riva, Pam, compiled: *Light from Silver Birch*, (London: Psychic Press, 1983) p. 201.
2. Schlemmer, Phyllis, V. & Jenkins, Palden, compiled: *The Only Planet of Choice*, (Bath: Gateway Books, 1993) p. 191.

3. Ibid., p. 191.

Question 35
1. Hodson, Geoffrey, *The Kingdom of the Gods*, (Madras & London: The Theosophical Publishing House, 1987) p. 56.
2. Ibid., pp. 58-9.
3. White Eagle, *Spiritual Unfoldment 2*, *(Liss,* Hampshire: The White Eagle Publishing Trust, 1981) pp. 25-6.
4. Ibid., pp. 26-7.
5. Ibid., pp. 32-3.

Question 37
1. Edwards, Harry, *The Power of Spiritual Healing*, (Guildford, Surrey: The Harry Edwards Spiritual Healing Sanctuary Trust, 1978) p. 106.

Question 38
1. *Kindred Spirit Magazine*, (Totnes, Devon: Vol. 3 No.11 Summer 1996) p. 39.
2. Ibid., p. 40.

Question 43
1. Malcolm, James, F., *The Nature of Man*, (Essex: Spiritualists' National Union) p. 23.

Question 48
1. Hodson, Geoffrey, *The Kingdom of the Gods*, (Madras & London: Theosophical Publishing House, 1987) p. 61.

BIBLIOGRAPHY & SUGGESTED READING

Bhattacharya, A. K., *Gem Therapy*, Calcutta, India: Firma KLM Private Limited, 1985.

Boddington, Harry, *The University of Spiritualism*, London: Psychic Press Ltd., 1985.

Borgia, Anthony, *Life in the World Unseen*, London: Psychic Press Ltd., 1984.

Cox, Peter, *The New Why You Don't Need Meat*, London: Bloomsbury Publishing Ltd., 1992.

Elliott, G. Maurice, *When Prophets Spoke*, London: Psychic Press Ltd., 1987.

Edwards, Harry, *Spirit Healing*, Guildford, Surrey: The Harry Edwards Spiritual Healing Sanctuary Trust, 1978.

Edwards, Harry, *The Power of Spiritual Healing*, Guildford, Surrey: The Harry Edwards Spiritual Healing Sanctuary Trust, 1978.

Findlay, Arthur, *The Curse of Ignorance*, Vol. I & II, London: Psychic Press Ltd., 1948.

Findlay, Arthur, *The Rock of Truth*, London: Psychic Press Ltd., 1986.

Foy, Robin, P., *In Pursuit of Physical Mediumship*, London: Janus Publishing Company, 1996.

Hodson, Geoffrey, *The Kingdom of the Gods*, Madras, Wheaton, Ill. & London: The Theosophical Publishing House, 1987.

Lacy, Marie Louise, *Know Yourself Through Colour*, Wellingborough, Northamptonshire: The Aquarian Press, 1989.

Leadbeater, C. W., *The Chakras*, Wheaton, Illinois: The Theosophical Publishing House, 1990.

Leonard, Maurice, *The Medium*: The Biography of Jessie Nason, London & New York: Regency Press Ltd., 1974.

Malcolm, James, F., booklet: *The Nature of Man*, Essex: Spiritualists' National Union.

Markham, Ursula, *Discover Crystals*, London: The Aquarian Press, 1991.

McClellan, Randall, Ph.D., *The Healing Forces of Music*, Rockport, MA. & Shaftesbury, Dorset: Element Inc. & Element Books Limited, 1991.

McQuitty, James, *Religion: Man's Insult to God*, Tarpon Springs, Fl: Tarpon House Publishing, 1997.

Naylor, William, Ed., *Silver Birch Anthology*, London: Psychic Press, formerly Spiritualist Press, 1969.

Ortzen, Tony, Ed., *Silver Birch Companion*, London: Psychic Press Ltd., 1986.

Ortzen, Tony, Ed., *The Seed of Truth*, London: Psychic Press Ltd., 1987.

Paine, Thomas, *The Age of Reason*, London: Watts & Co., 1938.

Polge, Coral, with Hunter, Kay, *The Living Image*, London & New York: Regency Press Ltd., 1984.

Riva, Pam, compiled: *Light from Silver Birch*, London: Psychic Press Ltd., 1983.

Roberts, Ursula, *Wisdom of Ramadahn*, London: Psychic Press Ltd., 1985.

Schlemmer, Phyllis, V. & Jenkins, Palden, compiled, *The Only Planet of Choice*, Bath: Gateway Books, 1993.

Sharp, Harold, *Animals in the Spirit World*, London: Psychic Press Ltd., 1986.

White Eagle, *Spiritual Unfoldment 2, Liss,* Hampshire: The White Eagle Publishing Trust, 1981.

SUGGESTED READING (Magazine)

==

For those interested in new energy physical phenomena, which is currently being developed and demonstrated, a group in Norfolk are producing a comparatively new magazine, they call it: *The Spiritual Scientist* (do not let the word *scientist* put anyone off, for all their reports are in easily understandable terms). I thoroughly recommend a subscription to this magazine. At present the magazine can only be purchased by postal subscription, their address is: The New Spiritual Science Foundation, Street Farmhouse, Scole, Diss, Norfolk, IP21 4DR

ADDRESSES

==

Greenpeace, Canonbury Villas, London N1 2PN
Friends of the Earth, 56-58 Alma Street, Luton, Beds LU1 2YZ
The Vegetarian Society, Parkdale, Dunham Road, Altrincham, Cheshire, WA14 4QG
Energy Science & Technology Corporation, 40262 Foxfield Lane, Leesburg, Virginia 20175, USA
The Spiritualists' National Union, Stansted Hall, Stansted, Essex, CM24 8UD

FOR ABSENT SPIRITUAL HEALING; MEDITATION, HEALING AND ENLIGHTENMENT TAPES & MORE

==

Please send requests for absent healing, or for a list of the author's cassette tapes, to the following correspondence address. No charge is made for absent healing, but donations to help with expenses, will always be gratefully received. Address: Jim McQuitty, Island Light, 36 Alfred Street, Ryde, Isle of Wight, PO33 2TS

RELIGION: MAN'S INSULT TO GOD

by James McQuitty

==

The above titled book is also available from the same address as shown for absent healing; priced at £8.95 inclusive of p&p., please make cheques payable to: Island Light.

GOLDEN ENLIGHTENMENT II

==

Further copies of this book are also available from the above address. For a current price list of all that is available please write; S.A.E. appreciated.